CAYMANKIND

MICHAEL C. FERRIER

CLMPublishing

Images: Cayman Compass.
Canstock. CLM Publishing

Published by CLM Publishing
Cayman Islands
www.clmpublishing.com

ISBN 978-1-948074-33-9

Printed in the Cayman Islands

"CAYMANKIND" *Moved Us*
So We Moved

Table of Contents

Foreword

This is a hilarious, informative, and easy-to-read book written by an easy-going, laid-back person who really captures the essence of our Caymanian culture; friendly, accommodating, and often described simply as CAYMANKIND.

Upon meeting Mike and Diana for the first time, I immediately realized there was something different about them, but also special; they were interested in getting to know more about Cayman, Caymanians, and our way of life. They were keen to know what drives us to be who we are, welcoming and warm to everyone we meet; what makes us tick and what raises our ire; and where we draw the line in the sand.

In this book, Mike occasionally wanders into dangerous territory, but knowing him as I do, I am comfortable that beneath the humour and exaggeration for emphasis there is a profound respect for Caymanians, matters of importance to indigenous Caymanians and our moral values; values that we are struggling to retain for the benefit of future generations of Caymanians.

With Mike's accomplishments in international business and marketing, having travelled extensively, and fluent in multiple languages, one might expect that he is experienced and qualified to know when he has found a rare gem. As a former Minister of Finance for the Cayman Islands, believe me that Mike is not mistaken; he found a rare gem and is hoping you will join him! However, truth be told and try as he might, his language skills have not adequately equipped him to correctly imitate our beautiful and amazing Caymanian dialect. Here's hoping you will do better.

This is Mike's invitation to those who might come to appreciate and share his love and admiration for the Cayman Islands, its friendly people, and their love for country that burns deep within their psyche.

Mike's book is very good, but to appreciate why he and Diana came and stayed, you have to be here.

Marco S. Archer

Foreword

I am objective about most things, except Cayman. This is my family's home for many generations, and we are better off when folks like Mike and Diana make it theirs.

"I like to shake it up every ten years or so" caught my attention most, when speaking with Mike for the first time on the phone. Thirteen countries in, at that time, he spoke as if he was in need of trying something new. Twenty years living within Monaco borders at the time, he was breaking badly his rule, so I had a hunch he would add Cayman to his list of life's starts and stops as his journey continued to unfold. Little did we know he would like CAYMANKIND as much as he does, making it his final destination.

I've been asked to write this foreword, mainly because Mike knows I'll say nice things. It is true that there is little wrong with this man. He's also asked because I know Cayman and Caymanians. My two kids are tenth-generation Caymanian – I grew up and live here. My great-great-grandfather was the last Caymanian custos, which was the governor equivalent of that day. On the whole we are a good judge of character, and a warm welcome is where it begins for most from abroad – and Mike's *CAYMANKIND* is no different.

After seven years of knowing Mike, I call him one of my closest friends, a confidante, and a mentor. Why? Simply put, he is the most interesting guy in the room, gives back to his community with caring, sage, and concise advice, always packaged in a way that only an adman of his calibre can, with an authenticity that is infectious. Mike is not only a professor in the classroom, he is also a professor of good living. Over his career, he's helped build some of the biggest consumer brands on the planet – his work spans the globe. And in this book, he has turned his unique experience of Caymanian kindness into words, which is important because it captures the essence of what people from other places have been enjoying for decades when they consider and move to our shores. The book demystifies what it is like to move here and to call Cayman home. It clarifies why this place is better than the rest.

In the pages that follow, Mike eloquently admires Caymanians as a welcoming people to those from other places and reinforces that this is our nature, which is one of the primary building blocks for our success as a country. Our CAYMANKIND culture welcomes those from elsewhere, from all over the world, in many different industries, and this migration of interesting and colourful people arriving from elsewhere has been happening for a long time. Mike outlines that in the '60s, '70s, and '80s, Cayman became a melting pot of different cultures who moved here from all over, who worked well together, and it's still happening today.

Cayman's culture is one of a kind in our region for multiple reasons, and this book helps capture it from a unique perspective. Given Mike's extensive travels and ability to call many countries home for lengthy periods, he is the ideal person to tell a story of unbiased comparison. Stories like Mike's attest that being kind and friendly are some of the cultural roots that have contributed to our success, allowing Cayman to thrive and grow.

Enjoy Mike's story. It's a good one.

Stephen Price

Foreword

Over the years, the Cayman Islands have become an increasingly popular destination for discerning retirees, as well as families and businesspersons seeking an outstanding quality of life.

As a leading immigration facilitator, I am often asked why Cayman is so successful, and what makes it so attractive to the numerous, wonderful personalities alighting upon our shores, not just to visit, but to stay. Well, here in this book, you have an answer.

The Ferrier family arrived on island in 2015 from Monte Carlo. Five families followed them out. In this light-hearted account, you will read why Grand Cayman was selected as their future home. What life is like here. What convinced them – and then their friends – to move. And stay.

Mike sums it up as "CAYMANKIND" – the title of the book and both a national slogan and the sentiment describing core aspects of our way of life. Yes, we are amongst the largest financial centers in the world. Yes, we are well-governed and offer first-world infrastructure. Yes, we have the Caribbean Sea and easy communications. But there is so much more.

To Mike and the others, foremost is the friendly, caring, and open-minded attitude of the Caymanian people. It has always been that way, and will always remain. It is who we are.

The Scottish poet Robert Burns wistfully prayed that a power be given to allow us to see ourselves as others see us. Mike expertly raises that looking glass to reflect unseen elements of our soul. It is much more than a good read. It is a roadmap, and an invitation.

Come check it out for yourselves!

Nicolas Joseph
Partner
HSM Chambers

Dedication

This book is dedicated to the people of the Cayman Islands and the welcome they extended to the author and his family. Including the help and support of my Caymanian editor and publisher at CLM Publishing.

Introduction

The Cayman Islands are largely unknown – or misunderstood. Yet here you have a relatively small, flat, and isolated group of three gorgeous Caribbean islands that have become the fifth-largest financial center in the world. Pre-COVID-19, they were one of the very few debt-free nations with a budget surplus and an annual growth rate of over 3%. Their average salary matches the USA and is by far the highest in the Caribbean. In a normal year over 600,000 "stay-over" tourists enjoy their facilities. They have two of the Caribbean's best hotels.

The Cayman Islands have achieved this remarkable commercial success without burdening its residents with conventional taxes. There is no income tax, no property tax, no inheritance tax, no capital gains tax. Practically unique in the world.

Wouldn't you expect a country of such commercial success to embrace a slogan that highlights these achievements? But no – the Cayman national slogan is a simple "CAYMANKIND." That's how they see themselves, and it is no sinecure.

They practice kindness. They promote it. They teach it. They revel in it.

They welcome 130 nationalities to their shores, and they show little or no chauvinism. The globe's high net worth residents walk around bejeweled but unmolested. Cayman has just about the lowest crime rate in the Caribbean. And it has demonstrated the fifth-most successful management of COVID-19 in the entire world.

The only other country I know which advertises the human condition over financial wealth is Bhutan. They measure their GDP in terms of "happiness." But Bhutan, for all its beauty and good nature, is far from a financial powerhouse. Cayman manages both. Fun *and* finance.

Is it a wonder that my wife and I added the Cayman Islands to our list of places to retire? Paraphrasing Julius Caesar, we came, we saw, and we were conquered.

This book is the story of why we moved, why so many joined us, and how fantastic and fun-filled our lives have become.

Read, learn, and laugh. It's a great story.

Chapter 1

Chickens Here, Chickens There, Chickens Everywhere

We decided to think about leaving Europe. There were a lot of reasons. The ever-increasing rents in Monte Carlo. The time zone differences and jet lag to call or visit ailing in-laws in the USA. Nostalgia for the Caribbean from days when I managed the area for my company. Maybe it was just wanderlust.

Or the persistent pressure of that banker who kept pushing us to visit "his" islands. And now. Whilst the real estate market was stagnating a bit. (More on him later.)

Whatever it was, here we were a few seconds from landing at Grand Cayman airport, and all excited. But then those seconds spread into minutes – and ever more minutes. The passengers started to worry. The American Airlines pilot must have felt the anxiety because he decided to open the intercom.

"Ladies and Gentlemen, you may be wondering why we are circling the Cayman Islands in a holding pattern – after all, this is hardly JFK airport or Miami. The truth is the tower has advised us there are chickens all over the runway and they are having a really hard time rounding them up."

I looked at my wife, and she smiled. The Cayman Islands may be about the most sophisticated of the Caribbean Islands, but, try as you like, you can't take the island life out of the island people. Cows rule in India. Chickens rule in the Cayman Islands. That's just the way it is.

As we walked to Immigration, the reggae band belted out the Bob Marley hit "Coming in from the Cold." How appropriate, flying in from drizzly London. The heat and the easterly breeze was a breathtaking contrast to the cold and damp of Western Europe.

And then we hit the stern-looking customs lady. "You got anything to declare, mon?"

"No, ma'am," I replied politely. The lady looked me over and examined my customs form.

"No alcohol? None at all?"

"No, ma'am. None at all." The lady examined the form again and turned to my wife with a smile.

"Is he telling me right, madam?"

"Aah! He's too dumb to be dishonest," she replied. Mrs. Customs was a little taken aback and then burst out laughing. The agent in the next bench looked over.

"Wassup, girl?"

"She sez he's too dumb to be dishonest!!"

Now the whole line up was in stitches. Thanks, Diana – now everyone in these blessed Isles will know their newest potential immigrant is a dope. Great.

"Where you going, mon?" asked the taxi controller.

"Sunshine Suites please."

"Good choice – enjoy yourself. That would be twenty dollars US – no more. OK?"

We walked to the waiting taxi – and another buxom local lady met us, big smile all over her face.

"Gimme those bags, mon. I can handle it. Where you going?"

"Sunshine Suites please."

"Good choice, sir. They say they do jus' tabout the bes' hamburgers and fish tacos there. Never tried them mi self. But that's what they say."

Goodness! Is the Sunshine Suites really so good or is its management paying off every taxi controller and driver in town?

The ride was a short 15 minutes. In fact, the entire trip from aircraft door to hotel desk could not have been more than 25 minutes. That was the first plus. The second was the excellent dinner at Casanova's by the Sea, a little Italian restaurant in the heart of George Town. Never eaten better pasta. And we had been seated right on the beach watching the circling, two-foot-long tarpons waiting to be fed. So far, so good. We smiled again.

In fact, we seemed to be smiling a lot already. And it was only day one. What would the next days bring?

Well, the first thing the next day brought was a decision to rent a car and take a better look around. I taxied back to the airport and surveyed the many rent-a-car choices. I decided on the one that claimed in big letters they were the cheapest on island.

"Well it's true – we are cheap. But not really that cheap." Grinned the big, heavy-set receptionist. "Whaddya want? A runt of the litter or a van? Ain't got much else right now. Almost peak season, ya know."

We settled on the small "runt" (a Kia), and the thinnest boy I've ever seen ran to get it, dropped in our cases, and held the door open.

"Try Coconut Joes for breakfast, sir. Most tourists like it best."

"I thought the hamburgers at Sunshine Suites were the ultimate?"

"For burgers maybe. I dunno. Never been there. But you're not here to eat burgers now, are you? So try Coconut's. OK?"

I tried to give him a dollar but he declined politely. "Part of the service. We may be silly cheap, but we try to be nice. If the car breaks down, call this number. But not after five p.m., OK?"

I took the keys and promised not to break down after 5:00 p.m. And off we drove to check out this new corner of the Caribbean.

::   ::   ::

The reason for this trip to Cayman was exploratory. In truth, my wife was not so sure leaving Monaco was such a great idea. After all, we had lots of friends there, we were well-respected, having served on school boards, been a charity volunteer, university professor, and helped the government whenever asked. Also, my wife adored Prince Albert and enjoyed many a fun banter with him at the myriad Monegasque parties. He even bought a sculpture of her for his garden by the palace pool.*(See more information on page 8.)

But she agreed to check Grand Cayman out. Why Cayman and not another island? I'll explain later. But for now, she remained sceptical.

I had a list of suitably priced properties to scout out before we met the banker and his wife and as we drove around, my wife got more and more excited.

"My God!" she exclaimed at one junction. "All those cars are waiting for you to cross."

In France, letting a car into traffic for no good reason would have you certified as insane. Here, *not* letting you in would have you judged discourteous in the extreme.

Opposite one prospective property was a major supermarket called Kirk's.

"Let's see what they have!" she blurted out. I tried to remind her that the purpose of the day was to shop for real estate, no other kind of shopping. But she was not to be deterred.

I sat in the car park, shuffling through my papers. Diana (the wife) came out of the supermarket flushed with excitement.

"Mike, there is nothing in Europe you can't find here. It's amazing. They have everything."

I grinned – as long as they had bread, coffee, and canned beans, that would be good enough for me. But I was happy she was happy. I think she was expecting a shop full of bananas and coconuts and not much else.

Next stop was a gated estate called Laguna del Mar. I had noted that Unit No 7 was for sale at a price we could possibly handle. To get to No 7, we had to pass No 5, where an old man was watching the waves from his rocking chair.

"Sir, where is Unit 7 – we hear it is for sale."

"Two units down – but why go there? My unit is for sale as well. Want to see?"

Well, why not? Nodded my wife, and inside we went. My wife adored it. In fact, she fell in love with it. We talked to the old man for hours, getting as much info as possible out of him about the beach, the life, the people, the ease of getting things done, etc.

He loved Cayman, but his wife had died recently of cancer and he just wanted to go home to his daughters in Kentucky.

Back in the hotel, I sat Diana down at the bar.

"Diana, that condo is way beyond our budget, and anyway, this is supposed to be just a recon trip. Don't get overly excited."

However, she ignored me. And ignored her earlier doubts. I could sense the cement setting. Uh-oh – I knew my wife. When the cement sets, that's it.

The next day or two we looked over seven condos at our budget level. Nothing matched the old man's condo on the beach.

"Diana," I kept saying, "forget it. *We – can – not – afford – it. OK?*"

Not Ok. The next day, she wanted to go back. Accompanied by the realtor, she looked the place over again. It had recently been totally redecorated with new bathrooms, kitchen, and furniture. Nothing needed to be done. No 7, on the other hand, was a total wreck.

Outside on the lanai, the old man raised his sad head and looked me in the eye.

"Do you want to buy my place? If so, tell me soon, as I head back home tomorrow."

"Look, sir, we are actually just here to check the Cayman Islands out and anyway your place – lovely as it is – is way above my budget."

"What's your budget?"

I told him – it was a full $450,000 less than he was asking.

"Are you offering me that price?"

"I suppose so…" I answered haltingly.

"OK – I accept."

I went inside.

"Diana, I think I just bought this unit. He is prepared to meet our budget."

"Good!" is all she replied. She was already working out where our own furniture would fit in.

The banker's wife was stunned.

"How much did he accept?" she demanded.

I told her.

"Can't be…no units here have ever sold at anywhere near that price for years," she replied, and went out to check with the old man.

"My goodness – you're right. He'll meet your offer. And it includes everything in it. Every last chair, bed, item of dinnerware, light fixtures – *everything!*" blurted the stunned realtor. "What a deal. What a steal! The rest of the owners here will be mad as heck – you just lowered the values of their units by thirty percent!"

Waking up to reality, I took my wife and the realtor to the Italian coffee shop just down the road – incidentally, also perfect.

"Diana, this was supposed to be a first exploratory trip only. We still have eighteen months on our Monte Carlo lease. We need to collect the money, etc."

"No worries," beamed the elegant banker's wife. Her husband, who had also joined us, grinned from ear to ear with excitement. "You can rent that place for at least seven thousand a month as long as you need and you will never, ever, beat that buying price. Even if you decide to sell it later, you can't lose."

"Diana, what about your doubts on leaving Monaco?"

"Michael, I have told you for years, I always wanted to live on an island. A Caribbean island. You know that."

"Really?"

I knew that! How come I never knew that I knew that?

Diana looked away in disgust – "men are so dumb" was written all over her face.

But I was cooked. I had launched a boat I could no longer control. Cayman Islands, here we come.

And what an amazingly positive decision that turned out to be! And what about that pushy banker and his lady? Can't thank them enough for what they did to enhance our lives.

* *In Monaco, Diana modelled for a local sculptress as a mermaid. Every detail of her body (above the waist, of course) an exact replica, full-size. Eight copies of the sculpture were cast (by French law that's the maximum for a work of genuine art). We bought one, Prince Albert the second, and the rest are scattered around the USA. Ever since, the prince called my wife "his little mermaid." For two years I tried to see it in place. Security always said no. Finally, during a cocktail party in the palace gardens, the prince let me see it. My wife wanted to know if the chest area showed signs of handling. It did...nice and shiny!*

Chapter 2

Why Cayman?

Before we get to discussing what life is like on an island like Grand Cayman, let's get the logistics out of the way.

Why the Cayman Islands? Why not any of the others? Was it just the bubbling banker? No – but his overwhelming enthusiasm certainly helped seal the deal!

There are about 30 different Caribbean countries, and often those nations are comprised of many idyllic isles. Think Bahamas: they have no less than 600 islands.

Most are independent nations – some are colonies (more politically correctly called 'overseas territories') or still closely associated with a larger nation. Think Puerto Rico, the US Virgin Islands, the British Virgin Islands, Turks and Caicos, the Dutch West Indies (Curacao, Bonaire, and Aruba), the French Islands (Guadalupe, St Barts, St Martin), Anguilla, St Lucia, Montserrat, and maybe even Bermuda stuck up there in the mid-Atlantic on its own. All some version of a dependent territory.

Then there are the fully independent nation states – Jamaica, Trinidad and Tobago, Hispaniola (Dominican Republic and Haiti), Grenada and the Grenadines, Barbados, St Lucia, Antigua, etc.

The choice is huge. Each offers a lot – and all have a lot in common. Great water, great beaches, coconut palms, fun people, and a laid-back lifestyle.

So you have to apply filters or the alternatives will drive you bananas – and I chose the parallel (bananas) carefully! Bananas and coconuts are, of course, everywhere. As for us, we wanted to be within easy reach of the USA and with direct flights to Europe to avoid the immigration mess in the US ports of entry. Cayman is one hour from Miami or Fort Lauderdale and offers four flights a week to London – Aruba, for comparison, is over three hours to Florida.

Then we wanted an income-tax-free regime – notice I said *income-tax-free*. Not tax-free. The Cayman Islands tax you (surprised?), but not on income. On most things you buy and almost anything you import. If you want to work there as an expat, your employer will pay an annual fee – anything from $3,000 to $25,000. That subsidizes the local work force entitlements. If you invest in property, you pay a not insignificant 7.5% in stamp tax.

But there are no ongoing property taxes. The Cayman Islands is one of only three nations in the Western Hemisphere to avoid them (the other two are Turks and Caicos and Dominika). No property tax and therefore, no forfeiture. You cannot lose your property. And any property owner, local or foreign, has equal property rights under the law.

Forget about accountants wrestling with income tax hassles. And possible deductions. It makes ordinary day-to-day life expensive – but so much simpler. The more you consume, the more tax you pay. The less you buy, the less you pay. Basta! Simple! And at my stage of life, "simple" is the name of the game.

In summary, the Cayman Islands are, to my knowledge, the only jurisdiction in the Western Hemisphere to offer total freedom from income tax, capital gains tax, property taxes, death duties, or withholding taxes on investments. Amazing – but true. The only one. And it's been that way for 500 years, so don't worry about any basic changes in the law. The Caymanians would laugh it right out of court! The local politicians know that to impose new taxes would immediately see billions of dollars exit the country before the ink on the legislation was dry. They may be politicians, but they aren't stupid!

Back to our story. Tax was an issue, as I said, but we also wanted an environment that encourages investment, a cosmopolitan population (there are over 135 nationalities living in Grand Cayman), Goldilocks-type land mass (not too large, not too small!), relatively crime-free, well-managed, with acceptable infrastructure, good governance, few race relation problems…and that effervescent banker and his wife.

The more you apply these filters, the more the arrows point to the Cayman Islands. They remain happily a colony (or to be politically correct, a "British Overseas Territory"), and are just about the most prosperous of all the Island offerings, with a population almost matching the average annual salary (62,000* inhabitants – $56,000 average annual income (see reference on page 12)), and only 22 miles long (9 miles wide). Small enough to govern easily.

As regards government, the Cayman Islands are pretty well controlled, with a respectable budget surplus (pre COVID-19). It has its own airline. Clean streets. And probably the best selection of fine eating establishments in the Caribbean. Could anything else be better?

Yes, something else could. The people. They talk about "CAYMANKIND" and they act it. People smile, they like to help you, they love to see you, they greet you in the streets, in the shops, and even in the government. What a contrast to the grumpy French or the surly Brits we left behind. Workmen stop to have a chat. Ladies give you a happy hug. Men shout a loud, "Hello, mon!" whether they know you or not.

It is truly refreshing.

Of course, the Cayman Islands has its problems. The government talks a lot and does a good deal less (so what else is new?!) Locals find it hard to find employment in the major industries of banking, hospitality, or investment, because education leaves a lot to be desired. A consumption tax regimen is harder on the poor. We have a growing drug problem. The occasional hold-up and a murder or two. But compare that with Bahamas, for example. *Cayman has less than 1% of the Bahamian annual murder rate.*

Most of us retirees live on the so-called Seven Mile Beach corridor, which – as its name implies – is on a wide stretch of sand almost seven miles long*** and the hub of most activity. Real estate on this magnificent beach averages up to $2,000 a sq. ft. – about 10% the cost of Monaco, where the only beach is man-made and polluted. (There are a few extra pricey new developments in Cayman that average $4,000 or more per sq. ft.)

Go inland and even near the capital of George Town, you can find a respectable dwelling for a third of that cost – and the properties will be clean, modern, and well-maintained. That's just the way the Islanders are!

So that is (in a few phrases) why Cayman was our first stop. Later, we had planned to visit Provo (Turks and Caicos) and Barbados, but we never made it. Grand Cayman ticked all the right boxes – so Grand Cayman it would be.

* *Growing at about 3% annually – goal of 100,000 inhabitants by 2030. Roughly 45% Caymanian.*

** *Seven Mile Beach is actually 5.6 miles long. The rest is in the capital, George Town.*

Chapter 3

That "Banker Fellow" and his wife.

I t's time to expose this banker chap and his relentless promotion of his country. When teamed with his super-efficient real estate wife, it was a combustible relationship. How did he (they) drop into our lives?

In Monaco, I was president of the Canadian Club. The banker worked as a high-profile investment advisor for a prominent bank. Monte Carlo seemed to him a good hunting ground to drum up some new clients. Through a mutual acquaintance, we struck a deal. He and his team would invite my club and other invitees to a dinner at the Royal Monaco Yacht Club, provide an interesting speaker, and he and his associates could sniff around the membership for prospects.

I got the better of the deal. Most of my members were Quebecers – if they migrated to the Caribbean, they'd head for the French Islands. But my wife and me? We were easy targets. As stated earlier, we already had the Cayman Islands firmly on our radar.

Jonathan (not his real name) stemmed from an old Caymanian family whose tentacles reached through many stratas of Caymanian life. The family was ambitious, successful, and wealthy. He knew Grand Cayman was right for us and the rest was history.

Jonathan and his wife did not force us to Cayman – but they made it very hard to say no. He will end up as prime minister (called premier) one day. It's a given. And we will help him all we can!

There are good people in the world. And better ones. This aggressive man/woman partnership is definitely in the latter camp.

Chapter 4

Getting There

Obtaining a residency permit looks straightforward enough from the Cayman government's excellent website. Just jump through seven carefully crafted hoops and the doors open. But as you jump, those hoops keep moving. We know the ropes now so we can help other hopefuls avoid tripping over them. My wife and I, on the other hand, tripped up badly.

Our doctor had to prove we were fit and she did – in French. Her report was translated. But the translation was returned. It had to be notarized. Proving we were financially viable was no easier. Our accountant – a USA-certified 28-year veteran – was not "acceptable." The police report stating *neant* (Latin for "nothing") was also returned for official translation *and* notarization. Our lawyers in Monaco thought we were crazy, or as the locals might say, "Duh wah you get" (serves you right!).

Our lawyers in Grand Cayman thought we were a little dumb too – until we got it! Of course – get the medical report, the X-rays, the accountants report, and all the rest "on island" and things go pretty smoothly, *and* the locals earn a buck. Surely everybody could work out the logic of that?

So we started again "on island" and whoopee, the authorizations came sailing through. Until we hit catch 22. You are allowed six months from the date of authorization to import your belongings tax-free. But you can only ship your goods when you actually get the certificate – the official letter won't suffice. That took another six weeks. Add on the shipping time (six weeks or so) and things could get a little tight. Even if things went well.

Which of course, they never do on Island Time.

There are at least 50 George Towns in the world – that king really got around. In the Caribbean alone they exist in Belize, the Bahamas, Grenada, Guyana, and, of course, George Town Grand Cayman. The most famous – or most infamous – of these is probably George Town Guyana (remember the place where Jim Jones, the cult nut, made hundreds of followers take the poisonous Kool-Aid?).

So where did our container end up?

You guessed it – twenty-three miles from Kool-Aid territory. We had visions of the Guyana locals trying on Diana's furs and riding around the jungle in my little Fiat 500. The bureaucratic complexity it took to get the container back on track again merits a book in itself.

But I couldn't stand the thought of relating that nightmare again. And you'd fall fast asleep as I recounted it. Boring. So move on.

At least the delay would allow us to do some redecorating. Diana decided she wanted the carpets ripped out and the entire apartment repainted a sunny white. Mr. Kentucky had favoured a duller beige. I asked the estate manager to recommend a painter – and I got a mouthful.

"Are you crazy? Pay those prices? Our staff will do it for three thousand – half what any company will charge." And true to his word, it was done. Quickly, efficiently, and economically.

But only after "The Cowboy" had tiled the floor – which was also completed in a few days with total professionalism and at a third the price of Monaco, or even Florida.

Nobody knows why he is called "The Cowboy" – not even he himself could explain it. And no, he'd never, ever, sat on a horse. "I'm 'The Cowboy,' and that's the way it goes, mon. Any worries?" he asked, fed up with my prodding.

I backed off. But I had another worry.

"Why can't they paint whilst you tile and save us some time?" I asked an exasperated Cowboy.

He looked at me as if I had just fallen off the moon.

"And have the tile dust stick to the new paint? I don't think so! Why don't you just pay it no mind, and we'll call you when it's all done."

We left with a little trepidation. I like to watch the workmen. Make sure it's all done properly. That sort of thing. As the Farmers Insurance ads say, "I've learnt a thing or two because I've seen a thing or two."

No need to worry – everything was done to plan, to time, and to price. This may be a Caribbean island, but it works like a German-engineered car!

The container finally arrived at our front door three weeks later with two happy, plump Customs ladies sitting sipping tea (our tea) and checking each case as it came out against the inventory. The car was the biggest hold-up. No one could find the VIN[1] number to check against the official papers.

"Look, ma'am," I kept saying, "clearly it's a FIAT, not a Ferrari. It's white, it's a 2012 vehicle, the license plate number matches, so what's the problem?"

---

[1] Vehicle Identification Number

"A car just ain't a car without its VIN; that's the problem, mon," smiled the sweating lady sweetly.

Tony's Toys (the one local garage that had actually seen a Fiat before) came over and showed us where it was. Under the car boot (trunk) carpet. And it was $120 for that, thank you!

After the VIN was sorted, things went more smoothly. The Customs ladies went for lunch (two hours or more) and by the time they returned, most of the other stuff had been unloaded.

They signed a few forms, welcomed us to CayMAN (the way the locals say it), and zoomed off to do whatever – probably cook dinner.

That was that, right? Wrong. They had forgotten to stamp the car papers. The licensing authority refused to accept the car without that stamp.

"But it's *signed* by the agent," I kept insisting. "Look, here is the receipt for the import duty." I showed them paper after paper.

All to no avail. A form is not a form until it's stamped. And stamped by the Customs agent that examined it. Another morning wasted until the shipping agents found her.

"Oooh, my Lord – silly me!" she beamed, and hugged me tightly. A bottle of rum may have aided her memory cells, my cleaning lady insisted. Maybe. Maybe not. We'll never know. I doubt it. Cayman is pretty incorruptible by Caribbean standards.

But whatever. Finally, the license plates were on and the car was legal. But I was not! I was advised not to drive it without a local driving license. You can drive as a tourist for up to six months on your own license. Once you are a resident, you are a resident. That 30, 40, 50 years driving experience counts for zilch. Residents take a driving test. All residents. Of any age. It's the law. So, back to the Licensing Authority we went.

The written test was a doddle. Sample question:

"When do you use your horn? To say 'hi' to a pal? To warn off the chickens or iguanas? When approaching a hazard (not a lizard)?" (I exaggerated a little!)

I got 34 out of 40 questions right. Hooray! I passed. I'm done!

Not so fast. There is a physical test still to negotiate.

"Don't fuss, mon. We'll fit you in today, no worries."

And they did. Two hours later. But they were two hours well spent.

"You takin' yo test, mon?" asked the local lady sitting and sweating beside me.

"Yes ma'am, I am."

She leant over conspiratorially and whispered, "I think they got that bald guy on today. Be careful and make sure you check his seat belt is fastened before you drive off. He caught me that way."

Well it *was* the hairless man's day and as we walked to the car, he asked if it was an official driving school car.

"No, it's my car."

Oops. No go. Insurance does not cover test drives in private cars. Come back another day or pay $50 for using a school car, which just happened to be available. I paid.

In the car, the inspector said officiously, "OK, mon. Leave the facility, go up Crewe Road until I tell you to turn back."

I started the car, put on the seat belt but did not move.

"Wassup, mon? I told you to leave the facility and go up Crewe Road."

I did not budge.

He looked at me as if I was mad. Or deaf. Or both.

I pointed to his seat belt, unbuckled. He smiled broadly.

"Oh, mon, you are good. Duffy no gonna catch you."[2] And off we went. Up the road half a mile, round the roundabout and back again.

All the way the instructor was extolling his sister's dry cleaning service and did I need a suit pressed.

"A suit pressed? In this heat?"

He laughed, signed the form, and I was legal. At last.

So now the car was legal and the driver was legal. But I had a problem. The Fiat was a Gucci model with cute green and red stripes around the car waist. The red did not like the Caribbean sun and soon faded. I ordered a new set from Italy and searched for someone to replace the old stripes.

Everyone recommended Rambo – a small shack of a garage off Eastern Avenue. Rambo, who was thin as a rake but forever eating something, took one look at the replacement stripes and hissed through his mouth full of rice, "Dem stripes no dang good. I'll fix it with me pal, the poster boy."

"But, but, but…" I remonstrated. "Those are official Fiat spares."

"They's official Fiat junk. Now, mon, you want me to help you or not? Don't kick up no fuss, OK!" I gave in. A few days later, there was the car – resplendent in the new stripes. The whole job cost me $500 – less than I paid for the Fiat replacement stripes. And the red never faded again.

I sold the car a few months later for a new Mini. A Canadian lad bought it and had the engine souped up. Everyone knew that car was mine and that I drive sedately. I received many irate phone calls

---

[2] You're no fool.

wanting to know if I was suddenly on steroids and why had they been cut off or overtaken or pushed off the road by this crazy nut (me!) driving like a maniac. It took a while for the truth to sink in.

Meanwhile, up West Bay Road, my friend – who had only just arrived – was going equally insane. No, not about his car this time. But about his prized carved mammoth tusk.

"They're ivory," hissed the pleasantly-plumped Customs lady. "That's prohibited by international law."

"Madam," my friend answered politely, "it's a fossilized mammoth tusk found in Alaska. It's at least four thousand years old."

Nope, no sale. She wasn't buying it. Tusks are ivory and ivory is prohibited. The African elephants had to be protected. The tusks must be destroyed.

"Madam, the animals have been extinct for forty centuries, there is nothing to preserve or protect. The ivory is *f-o-s-s-i-l-i-s-e-d*. They are from a *m–a–m–m–o–t–h*, not an elephant. An *Alaskan* mammoth that had no idea Africa existed. And even if it did manage to swim the Atlantic and trek across the Sahara to the central African Savannah, it would have boiled to death in that heat with that fur!"

Two weeks later, he got the tusk back. But he was totally hoarse from arguing!

But even he was relatively lucky. Pity the poor lady who had a bullet in her baggage. The x-ray machine caught it. She was a licensed California gun owner, and knew about the fanatically strict Caymanian gun laws. But somehow, a bullet must have slipped out of the ammo box and settled at the bottom of her case.

She spent a week in jail, had to pay a $1,000 dollar fine, and endured a 30-minute lecture from the judge. Her defence that a bullet needed a gun to be lethal had no judicial merit. The judge explained he was being very lenient because she was a lady, a foreigner, had a gun license at home, and looked rather pretty in her holiday dress.

Cayman supports and respects the rule of law. That could be one of the reasons why so many companies choose to operate from here – as we will examine further later. I like that as well, even though that California lady may have been a little harshly treated, in my opinion. Or the fact that two youngsters, a local guy and his girlfriend, an American, broke the COVID-19 quarantine restrictions and received forty-hour community service; however, the judgment was appealed and resulted in a four-month jail imprisonment. The message was, the couple deliberately and flagrantly disobeyed the law and suffered the consequences. The verdict sparked a news frenzy in the USA. *"Four months for a silly teenager? Disgraceful."* The lawyer for the couple appealed the four months and received a two-month reduction.

The stance Cayman took was admired by some and criticized by others, however, the news didn't affect the island either way as real estate sales seem to be enjoying the ride through the roof.

We may have arrived in a relaxed island paradise. And we may have started to get that island rhythm. But we also landed in a country that knows when to be serious. And just.

As I said, we liked that.

Chapter 5

The Pied Piper

If we wondered about our sanity and the rapid and seemingly frantic move to the Cayman Islands, our friends in Europe were *certain* we had gone mad. They tittered and tattled behind our backs for months – how could an apparently sane couple leave the wonders of Monte Carlo for – where was that again? "Les Isles Caiman?" Where the heck are they?" Even the prince swore we'd be back within the year and offered a 100 euro bet. He lost – but he never paid. Cheapskate.

Gossip turned to curiosity and then the e-mails started pouring in. Do you have a guest room? Would it be free on such and such a date?

First to come were our good friends from West Monaco (Fontveille). She was an Iranian beauty from California, and he a Swiss racing driver and entrepreneur. They came, they got excited, but two things got in the way. First, it never stopped raining that week. And secondly, his business was mainly in Italy, and the time difference would kill him. But to this day he wonders if he made the right decision. He still owns real estate on island.

Next came my brother and his wife. He has a medical consultancy in New Jersey and she is an accomplished painter. They fell in love with the place – but his wife, two ex-wives, six children, and four grandchildren pulled him back to the USA.

Shortly after my brother left, a recently widowed good friend came to visit and stayed in the Ritz-Carlton – consistently voted the Caribbean's best hotel. This is a very fashionable, elegant, and well-connected lady who hailed from Guildford, England, and Monaco. My wife was sure the "Island Life" would not be for her. She was wrong. One memorable evening, a few days before she left, she informed us in no uncertain terms that she had decided to come over and no – we could not talk her out of it. She bought a $4 million[3] apartment on Seven Mile Beach, sold most of her holdings in Europe, and arrived.

She is happy as a clam. She already has at least 20 close friends and hates having to leave the islands for any reason. She told the immigration lawyer, "My arm is black and blue." When asked why, she replied, "It's from pinching myself that I am not dreaming."

To us she added, "This is the only time in my life when I really do not want to go on holiday." My mouth dropped open – this lady loved to travel! My wife shut my mouth and hugged her happily.

Then the sceptical "hebes" arrived. He is a frantic and highly successful entrepreneur, and she likes the life in the UK. He laughed when we said we were moving to the Islands. "You'll be bored out of your skins." But he decided to visit anyway.

He was so anxious to check it out that we were not even here when they arrived, so we just left them a list of condos to consider buying and restaurants they might like.

When we met on our return a few days later, they had already bought a $2 million beachside apartment and loved it. Over dinner I blurted out, "But, Bud, you are a strict, practicing Jew – I don't think we even have a synagogue here. You'll be unhappy."

But Buddy was one step ahead. He had located a retired rabbi and had enjoyed dinner with him. Problem solved. He had already submitted

---

[3] At the time of writing, that apartment is worth over $5.8 million!

his documents for residency. And contributed a considerable sum to fund the proposed new synagogue. Today, he has bought three apartments in a new development.

Next on the list were a couple we hardly knew, but had met at dinner in Monaco once or twice. Without seeing the place (I think they may have spent one day here on a cruise stop) they had decided to leave Europe and buy in the same $4 million apartment block where our glamorous widow had found her dream home.

Again we endured a puzzled dinner.

"Chris – what are you doing? You have one of the best apartments in the whole of Monaco, paid for and worth zillions."

"Mike, we want to follow you and start a new life. You know we have had our marital problems and this might help sort things out."

Things went well for a while and then the old problems seemed to resurface. The husband left.

Now here is the really interesting part. The couple may have problems living together, but they hate being apart as much as they grated on each other's nerves when together. But both fell in love with Cayman, and neither wanted to leave. So guess the outcome?

They bought a second apartment right next to the first one. They see each other when things are good, they are neighbours when things get a little hairy.

How's that for a recommendation?

Then an old Swedish friend wanted to buy a Ritz-Carlton condo, but before he could cement the deal, his mother became dangerously ill. He is still planning to come next year.

And finally, a Parisian couple who had done remarkably well with starting a new style of television advertising agency announced they would come as soon as possible. They had eliminated the "French Caribbean" from their list (just like St Tropez – enough of zat!) but enjoyed our enthusiastic tales of Cayman life. They came and rapidly picked out a likely apartment block which they eventually purchased.

So, to add it up, that is at least four or five families who followed us here. The government started to take notice. They had issued only 30 or so residency permits *in the last five years* and here was this strange Pied Piper of Monaco dragging a whole army behind him.

The zealous banker and his wife arranged for us to meet the Cabinet. I told them what they obviously could not see for themselves. Cayman had qualities many frustrated Euros were dreaming for.

I told them they were losing out – other countries like Barbados, Cyprus, Belize, and Panama were attracting hundreds more wealthy expats. What a loss. High net worth residents were manna from Heaven. They fuel the real estate market, spend large sums of money, yet do not get in the way of the locals. They cannot vote or work. These residents are just pure gravy.

"So how do we attract more, Mr. Ferrier?" quizzed the premier.

"Start by simplifying the application process – it's designed to scare millionaires off."

"Harrumph!" snorted the premier. "We've only just rewritten the immigration law."

"So rewrite it again, sir." I told him how easy it was to enter Monaco if you could offer the right credentials. Then I compared our system with those of Panama, Malta, Belize, Antigua, etc. "They are way ahead of us, sir," I added as my final, parting shot.

I was escorted out.

Later, I asked one of the MPs who was present what the premier had said after I left. Had I made an impact?

"'Fraid not, Mike. The premier called you 'just another eager paleface trying to tell us how to run our Islands.'"

Well, I tried, I whined to the MP, and I turned to other things. I gave up.

But the relentless, almost crazed banker refused to declare defeat and now, some years or so later, the whole immigration system is greatly simplified, mostly along the lines we recommended.

If I helped a little, it's a thank you to the Islanders for having accepted us!

Chapter 6

What is the Cayman 'Angel Dust'?

OK, you still with me, dear reader? I know it's been a long time to wait before the secret of Caymanian charm is explained. What is this captivating "Angel Dust" that is so seductive?

First, it's the people. The Islanders. I already gave you a few examples. Let's add to that list.

One day shortly after I received my driving license, I went out for my early morning newspaper and coffee. On the way home, I forgot for a moment that Cayman drives on the left, as in England.

As luck would have it, I turned to drive on the right at one of the few places where Cayman offers a narrow, split highway. Facing me and grinding to a halt was a huge cement truck.

The driver jumped from his cab, put his hands on his hips and shouted, "Mon, you are really stoopid!"

As the traffic behind the truck backed up, the driver of the air conditioning van behind him ran forward to see what was holding things up.

"It's this stoopid man, mon! He be so wutless," explained the cement trucker. "'E dunno 'is right from 'is left!"

"So, let's help him get it right, mon. It's no good just staring at him, now is it?"

By this time, two more drivers had come forward. A big discussion started. Should I back down the road to the nearest opening? No, that might be dangerous to cars on the other carriageway. Anyway, Mr. Cement was obviously not convinced Mr. Stoopid (me) would be capable of reversing 150 yards up the roadway.

But our side of the road was narrow, bordered by bushes and ditches at either side and my car (an old Cadillac) was long.

"OK," decided the Aircon man. "He has to do a turnabout. Nutting else for it!"

About twenty-five turns left and right later, back and forth and back again, and we achieved the 180-degree turn. Everyone cheered. I waved, red-faced, and life carried on.

Later that week, I had to take a trip to Miami. I always fly Cayman Air whenever I can. I like them. And here's why.

On check-in, the lady looked at my passport and shouted, "Hey – it's your birthday next week!"

"True." I smiled back. "And what will Cayman Airways give me?"

"Nothing much, for sure. But I will." And she jumped over the weigh scale, out of her booth, hugged me tightly, and gave me a big, slobbery kiss on the cheek

The line behind me cheered. I was red-faced again.

On the way home a few days later, I had two suitcases full of stuff my wife ordered me to take back from our condo in Florida. Cayman Airways allowed (at that time) two checked bags free. But not two checked bags weighing over 60 pounds each.

"Oh dear," sighed the check-in lady. "What are we going to do about that?" Then a thought hit her.

"Are you a 'Sir Turtle' member?" (Sir Turtle is their frequent flyer program.)

"Yes I am."

"Then, sir, I will upgrade you to Biz Class. We have a light load tonight. Can't have you paying 'overweight.'"

When is the last time you heard an exchange like that from a so-called "legacy" airline? Forty years ago?

I have a bad foot and limp a little. As I was negotiating the steep stairs/ramp at Owen Roberts airport, a heavy carry-on in one hand and my cane in the other, the ground control man spotted my hesitancy, dropped the red bollard he was about to place around the engine warning passengers off, and rushed up the stairs to take my case off me. I tried to say "Thank You." He turned away saying, "Don't give it no kind, mon!

He did not even work for the airline – he worked for the airport. But he cared. They all care. That's one part of the "Angel Dust."

One morning I was sitting down outside my favourite coffee shop reading the paper as usual.

Across the road a big fellow shouted, "Hi! How ya doin'?"

"Great!" I yelled back, peering against the sun. "Sorry, but do I know you?"

"Don't think so," answered the big guy.

"So why are you greeting me, sir?"

"I greet everybody – that's why." And he walked on by.

I was trying to find Dr Roy's Drive in George Town. I drove around and around the maze of old-fashioned streets. Finally, I stopped and asked a passer-by.

"Sorry, ma'am, but would you know where Dr Roy's Drive is?"

"Yup – just down Fort Street a bit, turn left by the coffee shop. What you looking for?"

"The Fidelity building."

"Oh, that's not so easy. Here, I'll show you." And she jumped in the car.

"But you'll have to walk back in this heat."

"No worries – it's not far and anyway, I'm on my lunch break."

"Can I buy you a coffee?"

"Nope – you just gone clear now!"

Shortly after we arrived, we decided to take a boat trip around the North Sound. It was full of tourists happily slurping rum punches and singing with the guide. My wife, peering over the side, suddenly spied a big starfish. "Look at that!" she cried.

"You wanna see it, lady?" asked the guide.

"Yes," my wife answered sweetly. The guy immediately dove off the back (engines still running) and came back up triumphantly holding the fish. We had to yell at the captain to turn around and pick him up.

The guide showed the starfish to us all and then threw it back. "Can't keep it out of da water more than a few minutes, folks."

And off we sped again. The guide just did his dive because he wanted to please a guest. That's just the way these good folks are. And it's infectious.

Final example. One day, my wife had an appointment to renew her passport at the US consulate. Unfortunately, the secretary had given her directions from east to west instead of where we were coming from. I stopped on the curb whilst my wife entered an office building to try and find directions to the consulate. Suddenly a big, grinning Cayman policeman tapped on the window.

"What you doing on the pavement, sir? Move on."

"Sorry, Officer – my wife is asking where the US consulate is."

"Get her back and follow me. I'll take you there." And he did. And right to the entry canopy. We were at least a mile away.

"I love you!" called my wife as the police car eased away.

"Great – but don't tell my wife!" he yelled back.

So that's a glimpse of the people. A thousand times a day that little smile. That desire to help. That fun. As I said before, it's so refreshing.

Now what about the island itself?

Well it's warm, of course. Warm in winter, somewhat warmer in summer. Between 75 and 89 degrees F. There is often a breeze blowing and the sea is always blue, or azure.

Seven Mile Beach – where most of us live – has one of the finest stretches of sand in the Caribbean. Wide, long, and soft. A few feet offshore you'll see more fish than in your local public aquarium.

No sharks. (Well, there are sharks, but they mind their own business.) No jellyfish. (Well, not usually – after heavy rains occasionally!) Little beach coral. Unusually calm waters.

True, from June through November is hurricane season. You have to take care. But (touch wood) Cayman is not on the most common hurricane routes. About every thirty years we get really clobbered. The years 1932 and 2004 were terrible years. Grand Cayman being flat and low, wind-induced wave surges can totally flood the entire island. In both those years, most of the buildings were almost totally destroyed.

"It's very scary," a storm veteran told me, "but it's not all bad. Our shelters are state of the art – in 2004, only two people died. And the insurance paid for almost the entire re-building of the island infrastructure."

Another told me he rode out the storm on his top floor. When the wind abated, he opened the front door and water gushed in. Along with an 11-pound grouper.   \.

Summer can also see many milder storms and/or afternoon showers of the tropical style. Ten-minute downpours actually refresh more than they annoy.

Not least, throughout the recovery period after Hurricane Ivan (2004) the Dart organization just kept on investing in the Island future and infrastructure. The same thing happened during the COVID-19 lockdown. Dart didn't lose hope or focus. His developments stayed funded. (More on Mr Ken Dart later in Chapter 15).

The Cayman Islands are also one of the ten best diving sites in the world. The Islands are mountain peaks and only a few yards offshore, the walls drop straight down, hundreds of feet, affording an underground spectacle amongst the world's richest and finest.

Seven Mile Beach and George Town (the capital) are very cosmopolitan, offering shops of every description and over 60 eating establishments, from the simplest Jerk Chicken or Pork stalls to world-respected fine dining restaurants of every description. Fish, French, Italian, Indian, Japanese, fusion, fast food, slow food, tappas, or Thai. Whatever your heart – or stomach – desires.   Except Vietnamese.

It is not always cheap to eat out – remember that consumption tax penalty – but you generally get what you pay for. True, occasionally some restaurant in difficulties will try and rip you off – stale fish or (as happened to me) passing turtle meat off as chicken satés. As everywhere else in the world, these places die or management is replaced. But then again, Cayman has not gained the title "Culinary Capital of the Caribbean" for no good reason. Eat out and enjoy.

Outside of George Town is the new town of Camana Bay, built by the American billionaire Ken Dart I mentioned earlier. He richly deserves a chapter in itself (see chapter 15) – but suffice it to say here that it is a deep compliment to Cayman that this man, who could live and invest anywhere in the world, decided to pour millions upon millions into our Islands.

Drive out west and you pass one of the world's only turtle centre* (see more information on page 35), raising and releasing thousands of green turtles into the sea each year. Opposite the turtle farm is the dolphinarium – if you've never tried swimming with these marvellous creatures, here is where you start.

Drive on northwest and you are lost in the wilderness of dirt roads and abandoned beaches, called Barkers Reserve.

Drive east and you arrive at the East End – remote and romantic (see the Lovers Wall), with fantastic views over the shallow waters and reefs. Walk the beaches and find as many conch shells as you can carry home.

Driving north takes you (logically enough) to the wild and wonderful North Side, full of small beaches, reefs, and snowbird houses. Keep on driving and the road ends at Rum Point and Kaibo Beach. Both popular and family orientated beach eating areas. If you don't like driving, a fast ferry leaves every two hours from Camana Bay to Kaibo. This is where the better-off Caymanians spend their leisure weekends.

Just off Rum Point is the world-famous Sting Ray City which is an absolute must on the tourist circuit. Hundreds of rays swim around you waiting to be fed. They started congregating there as the returning fishermen of yore usually stopped on this sand bar to clean their catch. The rays caught onto the free meals, lost all fear of humans, and are now a treat to handle and fondle.

Recently found and recently opened are the crystal caves – a labyrinth rock crystal system of underground caverns, some of which are open for public view. On the way from there, stop at the Royal Botanical Gardens and see nature as God and the Caribbean originally designed it.

So Grand Cayman may be small, but it is rich in diversity and contrasting lifestyles.

And a bonus point – each clear day ends with the most dazzling sunsets I have personally experienced anywhere in the Caribbean.

And I've not even mentioned the boating, the fishing, the riding, the hiking, the flora and fauna, the iguanas, or the rare Caribbean ducks. Nor have we even talked about the two sister islands – Cayman Brac and Little Cayman.

If you want to know what the Caribbean was like 50 years ago, these two sister islands are the stop for you. Sea, sand, caves (a favourite for burying pirate loot), hiking trails, diving, and solitude.

The Cayman* Islands do not offer scenery that other islands cannot match. Only it is more accessible here, better managed, and its attractions easier to visit.

* *'Cayman'* is a version of the Spanish word for crocodile – 'Caiman'. Sailing ships would visit to collect turtle meat and replenish their water stocks, being careful to avoid the dreaded crocs. Crocs are gone. As are any dangerous species. No sharks. No poisonous snakes. No rabid dogs – the islands are rabies-free. We do have a few annoying flies. Mosquitos at sunset will be your biggest headache.*

Chapter 7

It's Oh So Boring!

Again and again our friends would write (at least those that have never visited) saying something like this: *"Sure – you'll like it now. The experience is new. In a few weeks/months/years you will be bored witless and wish you had LISTENED TO US!"*

Paranoia set in. Every morning I'd wake up and prod my wife. "Are we bored yet? Are you bored? Do I look bored? Are our friends here bored? Should we send out a boredom questionnaire?"

Every morning she'd answer. "Shut the hell up and let me sleep." She's no help in an emergency.

So I did my own questionnaire. To me and from an imaginary doubter.

Am I bored with the beach and having a great swim every day in the pool or in the sea? *Nope – not at all.*

Do I have less friends here than I had before? *Nope – just the opposite.*

Are our friends murderers, clinically insane, or depressed? *If they're "insane" it's usually because they all seem insanely happy.*

Is the weather depressing? *Are you joking?*

Do I miss something? Like good restaurants, coffee shops, supermarkets, four-star wines, good shops? *Well there's no 5th Avenue, Oxford Street, or Rodeo Drive here, but all I really need are shorts and flip-flops. Plenty of those stores. Name me a wine you can't find here.*

Do we have the theatre? *Yup – visiting thespians, local amateur dramatics. Top Broadway shows or English theatre fed into the local and amazingly modern cinema.*

What about society balls or visiting celebrities? *Well, quite a number live here (I won't mention them to protect their privacy!). And the better off almost all support or arrange charity events. Someone calculated that the Islanders benefit from over $100 million in charitable donations annually*** (See more information on page 39).

How about events? Concerts? Balls? Auctions? Charity balls? *Well, we don't have a philharmonic orchestra and/or a national ballet. But there are balls and dinners and wine tastings and visiting singers and goodness knows what. Too much, really. You could be out every night. And, of course, we have our own style of happenings. Like Pirates Week (mentioned later) or Batabano. What the heck is that? Difficult to describe really – it's a cross between a parade and a street party. If you like rum, being "twerked" by beautiful young girls wearing costumes covering as little as is humanely possible, you'll love Batabano.*

You won't find that event in downtown Tokyo or Toronto!

Do I miss the "big city"? *No. Everything I need is a five-minute drive away. I never have a parking problem. No pollution. No impossible traffic jams. No stress getting to the airport on time (another five-minute drive). No insanely expensive taxis. Little or no crime. What is there to miss?*

You don't have a queen or a president, do you? *No – we have premier (prime minister) and governor. We see them regularly. How often do you have tea with the queen?*

What about health? *I'll tell you a story about that later, but for now, note we have three hospitals – one national and two state-of-the-art private. And two more in construction. Furthermore, I rarely meet a person with a cough, a cold, or the flu. The island rapidly became completely COVID-19-free – one of the top five performances in the world.*

And sport? *Swim. Snorkel. Boating. Dive. Walk. Hike. Rugby. Hockey (field, of course). Cricket. Boxing***(See more on page 44). Soccer/Football. Horse riding. Even Bingo. You name it. And the standards (for such a little place) are remarkably high. If you like yoga and wellness centres, there are scores around the island.*

That may be true, but you can't get Sunday night NFL or major soccer matches on TV. *Nonsense – we have the same TV channels as any urban American.*

The locals will rob you, rape you, molest you, scratch your car, run off with your wife, dance all night in front of your bedroom, need deodorant, or go on strike. *Are you talking about Cayman or your own city/state/country?*

You can't drive to France or Italy or Kanas City. *True. But I can fly there, and Budget or Avis are very efficient, thank you very much.*

Aha! What about good investment advice? *We have branches of at least four major international banks here and two excellent local ones. They have access to the identical centralized experts as my banks had in Monaco, London, or Palm Beach.*

You have no direct flights to Budapest. *You got me there. We can get to about 10 American and Canadian destinations and London. But we do have an airport that takes about 10 minutes to check in and pass security. How long does it take you?*

It costs a fortune to import stuff. *True. If you must have a Rolls Royce or Ferrari, Cayman is not the place for you. But then again, you'd never get the Ferrari out of second gear!*

So, tell me again why I should be bored? Are you stumped?

Ok, a final point to note. You have family all over Europe. You won't see them. *True, I have three delightful daughters in France and the UK. Seven grandkids. And a sister in Holland. True, they don't come in summer. In winter? They fight over the spare rooms and stay for WEEKS!*

Then (as my wife so eloquently puts it) "Shut the hell up, already, and leave us a-l-o-n-e."

**One day I was irritated at the constant pressure from a neighbour to walk around town with a saving can to collect money for Meals on Wheels. I asked the lady how much the average can collected. About $150 to $200 a day. I gave her $250 and asked her to leave me to enjoy the beach. She thought I was mad.*

Chapter 8

Suitcases of $100-dollar bills

The Cayman Islands are not well known – one could say they have been so busy handling their business interests and building the nation into one of the richest in the region that they forgot about promoting themselves.

Meanwhile, other people seemed to have taken over the role of publicist. Especially a film called *The Firm*. In this famous 1993 movie, a young lawyer discovers that his new employer – a law firm in Memphis, Tennessee – is actually nothing more than an accomplice of well-known Mafia gangs helping them launder ill-gotten gains through dubious financial instruments located in tax havens. The tax haven chosen to represent the genre was, of course, the Cayman Islands.

Unfortunately, the film by Sydney Pollack (starring Tom Cruise) was very successful and the characterization stuck. Cayman is widely seen – still today – as the archetypical tax haven. Mention the country to the uninformed and that film comes up again and again.

Mention to someone that you moved here and they see you hauling huge suitcases of $100-dollar bills across the George Town airport baggage area and hailing a cab to the nearest bank run by the descendants of the famous Jamaican pirate Captain Henry Morgan (also known as Captain Blood!).

It's funny, really, and I'd be financially flattered if it were true. It is not true. Not by any stretch of Hollywood's imagination.

I was asked at a French Rotary**** (see more on page 44), meeting of some three hundred or more members to say a few words about where I was from. I started by asking the audience who could tell me where the Cayman Islands were located. One hand went up – it was a German. And he placed the Islands near Barbados. They are actually south of Cuba and west of Jamaica. Some 500 miles away.

Then I asked them if they had any idea what the Islands were famous for. *The Firm* came up a few times, and an Australian visitor mentioned diving.

The truth is much more prosaic. And if the subject bores you, just skip to the next chapter.

If you are curious, stay with me. The Cayman Islands *are* a financial centre – the fifth-largest in the world. And they are the domicile of choice of hundreds of hedge funds, financial institutions, and captive insurance managers. It is not a tax haven – in today's regulated world, you can't become a world leader in finance by burying untaxed hundred-dollar bills in caves.

The industry is highly regulated, and maybe even over-regulated because of the prevailing witch hunt of offshore financial centres. In the latest listing of top overseas banking centres, Cayman was not only in the top 20% but had risen 13 places in the rankings.

Don't believe me? Buy a ticket to Cayman, dare to stash $50,000 in your briefcase and try opening a bank account. What you will open is a prison cell, unless you have a very credible story.

There is one important exception. You can bring in gold or silver bullion free of restrictions or duties. Not jewellery – that's dutiable.

But gold or silver bars can be imported freely, stored, and do not require registration or reporting.

For two years or so I worked for my brother's company as a consultant. He paid me a modest monthly fee and expenses. The US government sent a team of auditors to check him out.

Of course the contract was properly executed and signed and the work completed as requested; the auditors went home again pretty quickly, tails between their legs. But it shows you the reputational legacy we have to fight every day.

Like many retirees, most of my income comes from dividends. Usually 33% is withheld at source as tax. My accountant in Florida keeps telling me I would pay LESS tax if I lived in the Sunshine State, as this 33% is non-recoverable offshore.

I prefer to live here. So I pay the penalty. Did you hear that, *I pay a tax penalty for living here!*

So why are those financial companies here? Because of the expertise collected over years and years. And because – as I have mentioned before – of the favourable tax regime based on consumption taxation, fees, etc, and not on income taxation. Any country can emulate this system – that they choose not to is their right.

Do we have our rogues? Of course we do. But so does New York, London, Hong Kong, and even Germany. Credit Suisse, Deutsche Bank, UBS, Wells Fargo, Bank of Scotland, even the Vatican Bank, etc. have all been hauled over the coals for tax or other infringements and charged massive fines. Just think of the mess created by "bundling" non-performing debt in 2009. Or Wells Fargo opening 2 million accounts in clients' names without their knowledge or permission. Abysmal greed is, unfortunately, a universal human failing.

Scandal has equally hit the odd Cayman institution or individual (think Webb of the FIFA organization) or the Caledonian Bank. But trouble is usually located and dealt with as quickly, or quicker than, many of our peers.

That is one reason we keep rising in the international finance centre ratings!

More interesting, maybe, is to ask ourselves how did these sleepy little Islands and their fishermen raise themselves to such international financial pre-eminence? I mean, as late as the 1960s, Grand Cayman was a mosquito-ridden backwater of a few thousand inhabitants with cows roaming the streets of the capital and almost no paved roads or telephones.

Largely, they can thank the Bahamians, and maybe, the Jamaicans.

After the Second World War, the Bahamas were one of the most sought-after offshore jurisdictions. Thousands of trusts and other instruments were registered there in the famous Bay Street companies. After Independence, Norman Island became the UPS-style transit point for South American drug deliveries, and the Bahamian prime minister seemed complicit.

The banks and their buddies fled in droves. They sought the reputation, or apparent legitimacy, of the Crown. Many departed for Bermuda, more headed to the Cayman Islands who, wisely, it now seems in hindsight, had decided not to join Jamaica in their independence quest. At the time, London had asked the Jamaicans to "control" the Cayman Islands. (I'll return to that story later.)

The Cayman government voted to remain an "Overseas Territory" watched over by the vigilant agents of Her Majesty. That picture of the Queen and the Duke of Edinburgh you see as you enter the airport is a reassurance bankers and clients respect.

To be fair, HNW (High Net Worth) or UHNW (Ultra High Net Worth) individuals obviously profit from the income-tax-free (i.e., consumption tax based) regime. But there is nothing illegal or shady about this. To profit from this benefit you have to live here, buy property here, and be here.

To argue that all the world's jurisdictions should tax residents the same, reflecting the prevailing rates of the highest income tax regimes (as some claim) is absurd.

If you want to bring those tax exiles back home, lower your tax rates. It's not rocket science.

If the income is generated in one country and you live in another, that (as I mentioned before) is taken care of by the increasingly lethal withholding tax impositions.

Enough said?

***Boxing is a little sad. The locals lack the aggression of their fellow islanders, like the Jamaicans, and rarely win. But they keep trying. One aspiring middleweight even arranges his own bouts, hires a hall and sells tickets door to door. I booked a VIP table for one event and took some friends and my visiting 16-year-old grandson. The table was ringside and sported two large bottles of rum. My grandson, being thirsty, poured himself a glass full and slurped it up. He was violently sick all over the car home and will never, I guess, drink a glass of rum again!

****Rotary is a world-wide organization whose slogan "service over self" urges its members to devote time to charity and community. The Cayman Islands - one of the smallest countries on earth - has no less than four branches. Three branches on Grand Cayman and one in Cayman Brac. I have visited many branches around the world. Few are more dedicated, happier or more fun. CaymanKind at work again!

Chapter 9

Sunday out East

aymanians are a social lot. They love to gather, share a beer, share a song, share a thought. Almost all are literate, and comfortable talking on their feet. If they can't easily share the price of a restaurant table, they will share a beach picnic, a jerk chicken or pork sandwich. Anything. Being alone is not their style.

Never have I been anywhere where the art of the brunch is more celebrated. The Sunday brunch, that is. Almost every restaurant offers one and the choice is endless.

The attraction ranges from relaxation after church or a chance to being able to have the whole family together (evenings the kids are – or should be – sleeping!) to a convenient birthday bash. Everyone can enjoy themselves and the host knows the cost is a set price for all you can eat.

Top of the list sits the Ritz-Carlton – at least $120 a head. But it is worth it. Plate after gleaming plate of anything your heart desires. Oysters and clams, other shellfish, salads, roasts, chops, sates, curries, the day's catch, desserts, and cheeses from all over the globe, and even a range of over 12 different after-dinner coffee concoctions. Don't plan anything for the afternoon or evening, and make sure your credit card can handle the check!

From the Ritz-Carlton down to the kebab stall behind the gas station on West Bay Road is a tantalizing range of alternatives. After a few months, we started to get it. Sunday is brunch day, just like Wednesday is mah-jong day and Thursday is "Soak Day."

Finding different places to celebrate the brunch ritual seemed a good opportunity to explore the island a bit. A half-hour drive from George Town (in the Breakers Area) finds you the Lighthouse. Run by a long-established Italian called Giuseppe Gatta, he and his chefs are some of the few who have mastered the art of keeping a heated tray of scrambled eggs hot, moist, and tasty. If it's not too windy, you can walk out and dine (if 'dine' is the right word for brunch) on the jetty and enjoy the sun and prevailing easterly breeze.* (see more on page 50.)

Further along the road east are a bunch of more local establishments, ending at Tukka's – a strangely incongruous Australian eatery hanging over the East End reef and offering the rather exclusive Kangaroo Burger. Goodness knows where that meat comes from!

Many restaurants also offer some local art for sale. Tukka's, on the other hand, offers American or Aussie licence plates cut up to make words like "Gone Fishing" or "Happy Birthday." My wife thought the artwork corny – but I loved it and immediately ordered a plate with the date of my niece's impending wedding. I thought it would make a nice, original remembrance of their big day.

Two weeks later, we wanted to go back to Tukka's to collect the tag or plate, but a friend called me and suggested we join them for brunch at Luca's – an Italian restaurant on Seven Mile Beach. I asked Diana to make the reservation and gave her the number.

"Hi," she said sweetly to the receptionist, "would you have a table for four this Sunday at two p.m.?"

"No problem – all arranged."

"And my husband wants to make sure the license plate is ready for pickup."

"License plate?" repeated the stunned receptionist.

"Yes, the one we ordered two weeks ago and you said would be ready this Sunday."

"Madam, this is a restaurant – we don't issue license plates. Go to the Licensing Authority on Crewe Road."

"No, no, madam," insisted my wife. "The *Australian* license plates – you know, the ones you make yourselves."

"Licence plates WE make? Madam, what are you talking about? I can't understand you. Do you want to have brunch here, or are you trying to renew your license?"

"Both, of course. Not renew – just pick it up because you promised to have it ready."

"Madam, please – Luca does not issue license plates."

Silence. Then, "Who are you?" asked my wife.

"The Italian restaurant Luca's on West Bay Road."

"You aren't Tukka's in the East End?"

"No – we are Luca's on Seven Mile Beach. And we do not do licenses."

"No licenses?"

"No, madam, no licenses."

"But you do brunch, right?"

I took the phone from my wife. Confirmed the reservation and nearly died laughing. I nearly died from the pillow on my head as well!

But Diana did seize the moment to press an idea she was harbouring but did not dare to bring up.

She sat me down. "You knew that I thought I was talking to Tukka and not Luca, didn't you?"

Not really – I had thought she understood about the change of plans. But enough is enough. I let it pass.

"OK, you knew. Now you listen to an idea I have."

This was the idea – only one a blonde could think up. On reflection, Diana considered that a lot of the stuff the old man from Kentucky left behind did not exactly suit her taste. Cutlery, crockery, sheets, towels, and goodness knows what else.

"We have a lot of stuff stored in Florida which we could use here."

Well, it was true that a lot of our "junk" we had diverted from Europe to our place in Florida, and only sent the "essentials" to Cayman. But now those "essentials" were obviously not enough.

"I checked," continued my wife. "Bringing what I want from Florida will cost over five thousand dollars. That's a lot."

I agreed with her.

"But I had an idea. You always wanted to do a cruise this year, so why don't we book one?"

"I don't follow," I replied. "What has a cruise got to do with your junk in Florida?"

"You're silly – if we take a cruise with a big cabin and that cruise hits Grand Cayman, we can bring the stuff down free."

"Free? But we'd be paying for the cruise, which will probably be three times the cost of the movers."

"That's not the point. You want to do a cruise, so that cost is already factored in. The stuff comes free. Why don't you get it?"

It's no use arguing – as I told you earlier, when my wife has an idea – when the cement sets – just give in, or sleep celibate. Which is not the average man's idea of what marriage is all about.

So we booked the cruise, packed four cases full of junk plus another for the trip and off we sailed. My wife thought it wise to warn the cruise director that we planned to leave the ship in George Town with four cases of household junk.

"My goodness – we don't have rights to offload passengers in the Cayman Islands."

"No, no," we exclaimed, "We will re-board, but we want to leave some stuff in our condo there. It's not a problem – we are residents, and the date is within the six-month free entry term for new residents."

The director hesitated, but agreed to talk to the Customs agents when they boarded to clear the ship for landing passengers.

The Customs men listened, laughed, and said OK – if they brought the bags to their shed for inspection,

We offloaded, struggled with the bags, and wheeled them to the Customs area.

"Ah – you're the ones importing stuff? Sounds a little crazy, but, OK, let's see what's going on!"

They rummaged through the four bags, slapped me on the shoulder and said, "Off you go – have a great day."

Coming back on board was not so easy. Now the bags were empty and a new Customs crew were on duty. Taking bags off a cruise ship may seem odd, but bringing four empty ones back really drove them wild. That made absolutely no sense at all. (But it did to my wife!)

Finally, after they had inspected every inch of every bag and tapped and prodded for false bottoms, they let us go.

"Couldn't you at least have bought a few bottles of Cayman rum?" asked the tired chief officer.

"We live here," we tried again. "We have a cupboard full of rum!"

The agent turned away; now he'd seen it all. Tourists – and new residents – are weird. And perhaps we are. But don't hold that against us!

Unfortunately, after 37 years, the Lighthouse closed in October 2020 – a casualty of the COVID-19-induced restrictions on visiting tourists. We attended the last (tearful) brunch.

Chapter 10

The Wedding – Combustible
Italo-Cayman Mixture!

By now I hope you agree that the Cayman Islands are a great place to visit or live. So maybe it would be a great place to have a wedding? Sounds like it. I mean, there is the sea, the sun, the romantic beach – and who wouldn't enjoy a few days visiting a tropical paradise?

My son fell in love with a beautiful Italian lady and they decided to marry. Actually, I think it was her idea. My son would have accepted a status quo, but you know women.

Because of green card requirements, etc., my son opined that if he wanted to keep the girl, he'd have to acquiesce to permanency and might as well do it immediately. They arranged for a quick town hall wedding in the little coastal town in Italy where she was born.

My son said it would be a simple affair and they would do the proper thing later. We grabbed a few clothes and hopped on a plane. My son met us at the airport just in time to drive to the town hall – but he forgot where it was. So we were late – very late. The mayor kept looking at her watch with that well-known Italian frown.

I did not even know I was to be a witness, nor had anyone told me what to do. All I remember was the mayor yelling at me in Italian and the father of the bride pushing me forward.

I signed a hundred documents and for all I knew I could just have signed over my entire wealth to the Italian charity of the mayor's choice.

"What now?" I asked my son.

"Oh, I think we are going to a little pizzeria or something," he answered. That little pizzeria turned out to be the most famous five-star hotel and restaurant on that part of the Italian Riviera. Even our dog had his own bed and menu printed out for him.

The food and the speeches and the singing went on for hour after hour as course after course was served up. I think six in all. And there I was in worn Chinos and a short-sleeved shirt. My wife was a little better dressed, but then she always is.

A wedding – even a hastily arranged civil affair – is not a wedding unless each and every guest adds six pounds in weight, gets silly drunk, and sings.

Well, my wife and I said to ourselves, at least it's done and he's well wed. Are you kidding? That was just the first act.

A wedding is not a wedding unless it also incorporates a church service. And this time, we would be expected to pay. Yoiks! We'd already spent enough biz-classing it to Italy at one week's notice.

So what now? A friend said relax, she had a solution. They had just completed a beautiful house built appropriately in the Italian style, and we could hold the wedding there. On the beach. In Grand Cayman (more on that house later). Their friend the Baptist minister would, they were sure, be happy to officiate.

Diane got excited. First of all, no charge for the premises. Secondly, of course few would actually come all the way to Cayman for the nuptials, so there would be enough room for all.

Wrong on both counts. Hauling tables, chairs, food, and catering 11 miles east to the mansion would cost a fortune. Secondly, she miscalculated the guest total completely. Instead of just a few coming, there were hundreds of acceptances from all over the world. Italy, Brazil, France, Canada, England, Spain, the USA, Holland, and Peru. Everyone (except my wife) knows that if Italians are invited to a party, they go. Wherever it is or whenever it is.

Clearly, the mansion would be difficult. The death blow came when the owners stated they normally went to bed at 8:00 p.m.; maybe this time they could stretch it to 9:00 p.m. – but that had to be final. (9:00 p.m.? That's when Italians finish lunch!!) Then the small band (led by a magistrate) refused to learn any Italian tunes. "Volare" and the "Tarantella" may be essential at an Italian wedding, but not normal on a Caribbean Island. How about reggae? Or calypso?

So we had to find a big band willing to learn those tunes *and* sing "My Way" in Italian – the bride's father's favourite song.

Then the Americans demanded to know where the rehearsal dinner would be. (Goodness, did we have to do that, too?) No one used the special rates we negotiated with two hotels and they were pissed because we promised "at least twenty rooms." (Airbnb would be cheaper and more fun – endless partying).

Two restaurants were quickly found. One (Luca's) for the wedding. And the other (The Wharf) for the damn rehearsal dinner. The only problem with the latter was they had scheduled a divorce party for the same day, and was that OK? If that was the bad news, the good news would be that we could share fireworks and steel band costs with the deliriously happy divorcee.

"OK, OK," I said, defeated, "just don't tell the Italians that half the eaters in the restaurant were celebrating divorce. Italians are superstitious." But everyone got so drunk they would never have found out anyway!

The weatherman was another disappointment. At first he promised sun, but changed his mind and forecast rain – and a lot of it. Crap – who could supply tents at the last moment? Well, many, if you were prepared to pay the last-minute price-gouging rates. What other choice did we have? My broody and negative friend was sure they bribed the weatherman; the sun shone almost all day.

Then the testy French all refused to go on the chartered ferry lunch excursion to the beach restaurant – they thought they'd eat better in the condo. They had spent all morning agreeing on the menu. Oh, the French – bullied by their bellies.

The last straw? Would you believe this? On the wedding morning, the BMW dealer just had to choose that day to deliver the new Mini I had ordered months before but had never told my wife. She thought it was a rented limousine and beat me over the head with a conch shell.

"Are you crazy? Two midgets won't fit in that." I couldn't explain, as I had to rush off. One of the guests – allergic to shrimp – had eaten something with shrimp in it and was dying.

Left alone, the harpist now looked lovingly at all the half-poured bottles of Prosecco and wanted to start playing jazz during the service. I had to physically restrain him.

And the groom, egged on by his lunatic best men, thought it hilariously funny to slap a piece of creamy wedding cake in his wife's face. She nearly decided to join the divorce party there and then (Italians are so emotional).

The father of the bride never arrived (he was ill) but the band kept playing "My Way" anyway (since they had taken the trouble to learn it). And the restaurant refused to serve any more liquor after 1:00 a.m. (The religious service was at 11:00 a.m.!) The Italians danced on regardless that the music was gone and the booze taps switched off (they couldn't fit another ounce in their bellies anyway). How do you stop these Italian Energiser bunnies? I led them out by arranging a conga line all the way to the waiting and fast asleep bus driver. The minute the last drunk conga'd out of the restaurant door, we slammed it shut. Basta!! Enough already. They carried on conga'ing in the bus. Probably until breakfast, as far as I know.

I was exhausted. But the group universally voted it the best wedding they had all ever attended. That's the magic of Cayman for you. It can all go wrong, but it never goes wrong. Who cares when you have a turquoise sea, fine food, endless supplies of Caribbean rum, and the happiest locals in the world to smile at you? Plus a bunch of uncontrollable Italians.

Another reason for the success? Because of all the languages present (Italian, French, Spanish, Portuguese, Dutch, German, English), my wife had dictated "no speeches" at the main event. A wedding with no speeches is the only way to go. I know that now. More time to sing, dance, and slurp alcohol. Remember that if you are planning your own wedding. Or divorce.

Chapter 11

Cayman Industries

OK, you finally decided to visit Cayman and you are looking for souvenirs to take home. What's the choice?

Well, if you are male, how about a Caymanian woman? They have the finest, largest, roundest behinds in the Caribbean. *"It's de cushion for de pushin',"* as my Cayman gardener pal informed me.

If that's a little over your budget, you can look for our version of Caribbean rum. The most expensive is called Four Fathoms Deep because the distiller was out of warehouse space and decided to let the rum age at the bottom of the sea in barrels.

The movement of the waves turning the barrels gives it a rather unique taste. The locals have been trying to find out where the barrels are laying for years. So far, no luck. Maybe it's a myth.

Then you have Tortuga rum and their famous rum cakes in various flavours. They are everywhere, and they are expensive. It's a pretty average cake splashed with a spoonful or two of their prime rum. Tourists love the cute little six-sided boxes.

The most idiotic rum brand is called Big Black Dick rum. I gave a bottle to my urologist in London and he cherishes it. Was the title deliberate double entendre or were the owners unaware of the irony?

The "Black Dick" supposedly refers to the French pirate Richard le Grand, who was thrown off a ship and swam a reported twenty miles to the Cayman Islands. The small mini-bottles were the most stolen item by ladies at the airport duty-free.

Then we have "Caymanite" – a unique rock formation only found on Grand Cayman or Cayman Brac. The locals sculpt anything out of it – stingrays, dolphins, starfish, or many smaller jewellery pieces. The items are not cheap – the rock is hard to work. But the colour combinations of grays, oranges, and whites can be quite breath-taking.

If you feel the need to clean out your bowels, go for any one of myriad pepper jellies or sauces. The Mexicans have to eat jalapenos with everything – or die. Similarly, the Caymanians sprinkle this lethal pepper *poison* on all they eat. They learnt it from the many Jamaicans who visit. All have holes permanently burnt in their tongues. Avoid accepting a passionate kiss from a Caymanian after a meal!

Finally, if your country allows you to import raw or cooked meat, how about a pound or two of turtle steak? Caymanians love it and farm it. Well-cooked by someone who knows what he or she is doing, and it's tasty. Otherwise it can be tough and a bit fishy.

If you were here a few years ago, you could have collected a bargain. A local entrepreneur decided he'd become the T-shirt, polo shirt, baseball cap, and carry bag centre of the Caribbean. To get good prices he ordered millions of dollars of merchandise, branded them "Caribbean Canvas," and waited to get rich. He went broke. The enormous stock was sold off over months, sometimes at prices as low as one dollar an item. I've given tons to happy friends and relations. (But I don't tell them what I paid!!!)

Of course, we also have many very talented artists and over 130 local authors – you are reading one here. But if you are going to publish on island (we have two local publishers), take care. This is a Christian country. The publishers reserve the right to edit your work. "You ass" becomes "You big back side." "You fu---r becomes "You fugger." "Horny" becomes "hormone-filled." "Shit" equals "Shoot." It can change the sense a little. "Stop shitting me, you ass" may end up as "Stop shooting me, you big back side." Somehow, "I don't give a fig," doesn't quite have the snap of "I don't give a f—."** (see more on page 59)

If you are here for Pirates Week, you or your kids will have fun with all the pirate paraphernalia on offer. My first Pirates Week I sat on the jetty next to an empty chair. I did not know it was the chair the governor would be sitting on when the pirate ship arrived and kidnapped her (it was a female governor at the time). It's a happily anticipated event – and it happens every year. Curiously, the pirates fly in from Seattle by Boeing – not on a ten-sail ship. Nope, nobody knows how Seattle achieved that honour.

I was in the doctor's office a few days later and this woman came in for an appointment. She looked familiar, so I leant over and asked stupidly, "Madam, do I know you?"

"Yes, I am the governor, and you watched me being kidnapped last week. A gentleman would have saved me."

Was she joking? Not sure, as the doctor called me in at that moment.

If you can stand the weight penalty, we have some pretty good beers in six packs to take home. Caybrew – a light, gay lager – is the most popular. Ironshore is deeper and darker, but equally tasty. Caybrew is what you sip as you listen to karaoke in the many bars we have around the islands.

The atmosphere is usually warm and the welcome friendly – locals like to mingle. The karaoke is a little more difficult to bear. A friend from Rotary asked me to join him for a karaoke sing-along in Murphy's pub. He selected "Fly Me to the Moon" as his contribution to the evening's cacophony. But when his name was called, he froze with stage fright. A famous politician was watching from the other side of the bar. My friend pushed me to take his spot. I am awful; I sound like a 20-year-old diesel engine. I was sure I'd be kicked off the island.

I smiled at the "Honourable" as I regained my seat. He smiled back. "You are invited to my next barbecue. Your singing will keep the mosquitos away." Nice guy. Lucky for him I can't vote.

Not your normal Cayman reaction. The locals, as I have repeatedly stressed in this book, are painfully polite. At a famous four-way stop in West Bay you can wait for hours as each driver urges the others to go next. They all start, stop, wave again, all start again, all stop again. It can "drive" you insane. (Sorry about the pun!!)

** *My island-edited "swearing" or intimate scenes enraged an author friend of mine called Gay (who is not gay, by the way), who called my sex scenes amateuristic and juvenile. She challenged me to write a "real story, and from the woman's point of view," and if she liked it, she'd get it published off island. She's 60 years old. The edited version shocked the devil out of me. Pure porn. Now what do I do? I have three daughters. Maybe I'll publish under a pseudonym? But not in the Cayman Islands. As my publisher continually reminds me "yo mout don't join church?!"*

Chapter 12

Is Cayman a Good Place to Retire?

I s the Cayman Islands a great place to retire? Are you kidding? Is the sky blue? Or the Caribbean aqua? Of course it is. Let's go over it again. Sea, sun, and sand. Good infrastructure. Great health facilities. Modern housing. Multi-national population. The friendliest locals. No race bias. Very little crime. A great airport not far from Miami (one-hour flight). And plenty of fantastic restaurants.

True, the Cayman Islands is not cheap. The cost of living is high, thanks in part to the consumption tax regime. Housing is not inexpensive either. If you want to live on Seven Mile Beach, on the beach, calculate $1.000 a sq. ft. at least. Up to over $4,000 for prime property.

But then again, I repeat, there is no income tax, no property tax, no death duties, and no duty on necessities. So – yes – you have to have a certain income, or perhaps try Panama or the Dominican Republic, for example.

Ergo, if the place is a magnet for the wealthy to hang their hats, therefore – surprise, surprise – you find a few here. In fact, every year more and more.

Like everywhere else that attracts the well-off retirees, we have our recluses – like Ken Dart or Mark Cuban (well, he's not really retired yet). And we have the eccentric. Rather a lot of them. Collectively and individually, they keep us smiling.

A few examples.

The faux Italians. Let's start with the delightful couple who gave up their citizenship and decided they were Italian and that Cayman deserved a couple of acres of Italian architecture. Neither of them knew much about Italy then (they do now), nor did they speak a word of the language. And yet they talked themselves into Italian passports, absorbed Italian renaissance architecture, and flew to China to create the most fabulous copy of a renaissance Italian mansion in the Americas, all carted over in 197 containers from various cities of the "Middle Kingdom." Tour buses stop by the gates and mouths drop open. I mentioned the property earlier when relating the story of our "Italian" wedding. There are over 30 statues alone!

An incredible achievement.

Next, let me introduce to you the British foghorn, who must have lived somewhere in the mistiest part of those cloudy isles. She never talks – she shouts. Blasts your eardrums off. And her laugh shakes you into a coma. Har! Har! Har! I love her. It's infectious. She laughs – we all laugh. Or die from decibel poisoning.

And there are many more – but most are friends or acquaintances and might recognize themselves. So let me just save the space to concentrate on the most loveable and most looney of them all – Nutty Nick. (Not his real name.)

Nick retired many moons ago from building a highly successful mail order business in Europe. He lives in a large house on the water and has found himself a beautiful, young Oriental wife. So far, so good.

But Nick never paid his dues to the gods of accident avoidance. If anything will happen to anyone, it will happen to him.

Nick took his visiting friends from Europe to one of his favourite eateries in the East End. A restaurant that feeds the frigate birds with offal twice a day. Timing their arrival exactly right, Nick dons the glove like a professional and holds out the fish for the huge birds to swoop down and whisk away.

Everybody claps. Until bird number five zooms down overhead and offloads a pound and a half of guano right on Nick's bald head. The crowd cheers. What an expert to get a bird to do that!

Nick's wife panics. Nick has had a liver transplant and he has been warned to stay away from bird poop. It contains toxic bacteria dangerous to a compromised immune system. Nick is rushed to the men's room and his head forced under the faucets. Now he is dripping wet with poopy remains dripping all down his shirt and he's petrified his days on Earth may soon be over. They're not. Nick will live to trip up another day.

That next adventure happened just a few months later. Nick and his wife decided to sell their boat and buy kayaks instead. At the marina, as his wife was settling the financial affairs, Nick spied a ceramic knife display and took one out of its sheath. Nice, thinks Nick, at last a seaman's knife that won't rust. After completing his examination, Nick tried to replace it in its holder. Instead, he nicked his thumb. It was a tiny cut but Nick was on blood thinners. Blood spurted out everywhere. Nick took one look and fainted, pinning his wife to the floor.

Someone called an ambulance whilst the marina tried to find a plaster. When the ambulance arrived, they asked to see the cut, now Band-Aided with a small plaster.

Nick ripped off the covering, saw the blood and – yup, you guessed it – fainted again. As he was coming around, the ambulance men decided there was nothing life-threatening and prepared to leave.

"You going downtown?" asked Nick. Of course they were. So Nick asked to be given a lift. The two paramedics thought Nick was off his nutter and strapped him to a gurney and rushed him to the hospital, sirens blaring. There, the nurses rushed him to emergency and asked where the wound is.

Once again, Nick proudly shows the half-inch cut, goes gray and – whoops – passes out for a third time. This results in a two-hour hospital examination.

Finally released to a furious and deeply embarrassed wife, the couple drove home to reunite with their guests.

Proudly, Nick showed them the tiny plaster, slowly took it off dramatically, and – bang – he was on the floor for one more dramatic performance, but this time he bumped his head. The ambulance men rushed back.

"Oh no, not him again!" one yelled as the other prepared the gurney for another free ride downtown.

Then there was the time he was stung by a jellyfish and demanded that all the tourists standing around pee on him, until a holidaying nurse corrected him. You do that for sea urchins, not jellyfish. (Actually, I am not absolutely sure it was Nick or a cruise tourist!)

Or the day Nick tried to return three bags of cement to Home Depot in Florida (worth thirty dollars), costing goodness know how much more in overweight and endless hours trying to explain things to three very curious Miami customs officials.

Nick keeps us amused at the "Romeo" club lunches. What's that? you ask. R>O>M>E>O stands for "Retired Old Men Eating Out." Membership is restricted to eight. Rejected applicants started their own competition. Such as Craft. "Can't Remember A Frickin Thing."

It didn't last long. To accommodate the crush, Nick opened a second lunch day. Now 16 old men giggle away every week.

And the older ladies? Well, they have their mah-jong days, their "Floaty days" (floating with champagne in someone's pool), and charity drives.

So, yes – the Cayman Islands is a good place to retire. It's a friendly place, and people are happy. Young or old, Cayman is a happy place.

What more is there to say?

Chapter 13

The COVID-19 – Cobblestone Complex

So far, we've largely concentrated on the good news and the advantages of a relocation to the Caribbean, and especially the Cayman Islands.

We moved and loved it. Many followed us and enjoyed it. Then some started to get what I called "The Cobblestone Complex" and started getting nostalgic about where they came from.

The Brits forget the cold winds, the dreary winters, the grumpy populace, the taxes, and the incompetence of the administration. They miss the theatre, the Buck house parties (although I've never met anyone who has actually attended one!), the ability to "visit the continent" at will, or having that Sunday roast with relatives (who they tried to avoid before). They start fantasizing about "the old roads, buildings – the history." Or what two of these unhappy refugees called "the cobblestone streets" although – again – where is there one left in the UK?

The Monegasque (those from Monte Carlo) miss Prince Albert (whose hand they once shook), the Grand Prix (whose noise they hated and fled), the Yacht Club (whose over-priced and underappreciated food they constantly criticized), the ability to have a pizza and buy fake designer handbags in Italy, etc.

It's an almost universal affliction. Mostly it dissolves when they pay a visit "back home" and they calculate the taxes, the crowds, and costs of a lousy meal, the takeover by the Russians (in Monaco) and the foreigners from the Middle East in the UK, the lousy traffic, the dirty public transport.

But for a few, the condition is fatal. To be fair, it is hard to compare the Cayman Islands with, say, France. Here we have a population of just 62,000, two amateur theatres, one cinema, no queens or princes, no fashion shows, no Louvre or British museum, no Chartres or Canterbury Cathedrals, no 34 native cheeses or thousands of local wines (against just a few rum brands), a vast range of landscapes (versus an island of just 22 miles width), easy (and cheap) flights to scores of different cultures and a feeling you are at the centre of "the happenings" and can drive from beach to ski resort in about two hours.

And then we had the COVID-19 pandemic in spring 2020. Boy, did the nostalgia dissipate in a heartbeat. It hit us in early March as a cruise liner raced a patient to one of our hospitals with a suspected heart attack. Unbeknown to the hospital staff, he also had COVID-19 and died a few days later. From that incident, the virus spread quickly.

The government did not hesitate. On March 20, 2020, the airports and ports closed, draconian lock-down conditions were imposed, throwing over three thousand onto the unemployment lines. Luckily, the government had operated for some years in a surplus and was able to pay the workless a stipend. Locals were able to cash in part of their accumulated pension contributions. A chartered aircraft (paid for by a wealthy resident) collected 150,000 COVID-19 test kits from Korea, of which 30% were sold on to other islands.

At the peak, about 280 cases were detected by the ambitious testing program until about July 20, when the three islands were declared virus-free. The fifth-best containment performance of the 180 or so countries invaded by the Corona bug.

Now the trick becomes, of course, how do you re-open the borders and avoid a second wave? That will not be easy, as one of our prime feeder markets is the USA, where the pandemic is definitely not under control at the time of writing. But penalties for non-compliance are fierce - as the story of the 18-year-old quarantine breaker demonstrated.

The government did its job, but that is only half the story. The other half is the people. They listened. They followed their leader's advice and they took care not to infect their fellow citizens. Being kind and caring of your neighbour is part of their culture and is deeply embedded in their nature.

Where does this caring and lack of friction come from? I often ask my Caymanian friends that question. The answer seems to be linked to the common heritage.

In the early years of settlement, quite frankly, the islands were a dump. Flat, swampy, and humid. The mosquitos were so bad, cattle could not be imported. They all died from being unable to breathe – so many mosquitos would invade their nostrils. If the mosquitos didn't bite you to death, maybe a hungry crocodile might (the Caiman type from which the islands get their name).

The few hundred settlers who braved it out had slaves, as elsewhere in the Caribbean. But when conditions are so atrocious, everyone has to pull together or quite simply die. As a Caymanian friend summed it up, "Life is best when one hand washes the other!"

Slaves and owners forgot their different status levels and learnt to live and work as one team. Even then, the land was not conducive to good farming or husbandry.

The only way a family might get enough money to survive was often to send the men out to sea either in fishing boats or transporters. With no men to help run the household, the neighbours all rallied round and looked after each other. Colour (Black, white, or Caribbean coffee) didn't enter into the equation. Common survival was the order of the day. As they say, "Necessity breeds strange bedfellows."

And from where do the islands get their tax-free status? That's another telling anecdote. In 1794, a convoy of ships left Jamaica for the USA and Britain. In a severe storm, 10 ships floundered on the reef off Gun Bay on the eastern side of Grand Cayman. Despite the foul conditions, the islanders swam out and saved most of the sailors, many of whom could hardly swim. Amongst those saved (says the folklore) was the son of the reigning monarch.

The King of England was so grateful and impressed, he granted the Islands two rewards. First, they could never be conscripted into any of the Empire armed forces (unless they wanted to join up). And secondly, they would never be taxed.

When Jamaica declared independence on August 6, 1962, the Cayman Islands were asked if they wanted to continue a political union with their newly independent neighbours.

What? And lose the right to a tax-free future? No thanks, we'll go it alone. And as you read earlier, make it alone they did.

Again, the economic success can be explained in many ways by the Caymanian character we mentioned earlier. Keep cool, mon. Talk it out. Evolution not revolution. Let's sit down and "fass it out" (*talk it through*). Rather like an Asian culture, losing your temper means you can't think of a better way to win the argument. And it is arguments that rule – not rants.

Watch their parliament meet and talk. It's endless, off the cuff ramblings until the Speaker of the House falls asleep. Regularly. But in the end it gets done, and the staunchest opponents will hop off together for a rum and Coke or a Caybrew after what they might have called 'a fearsome debate.' Fearsome? I've never heard one raised voice – ever.

People here don't dislike each other. They just avoid those who see things differently. "Hey, mon, you only got de one life. Enjoy it, mon."

And it all starts at school. The kids are taught to be nice and polite. I was in our one and only Starbucks the other day. I happened to have ordered exactly what the two young students behind me also ordered. Medium-size strawberry Acai. I grabbed the first one to come out. The barista cried, "That's not yours – it's the lady's!"

"What?" I cried. "But I was here before them."

The barista did not understand through my COVID-19 mask. I shouted louder. The girl dropped the cup back on the bar and said, "Here – please take it, please. We can wait."

Imagine that scenario in Paris or Rome. "O la la – zute! C'est pas possible. Mais non. Quel horreur." Right?

Caymanians by and large are relaxed and nice. Exception if the subject of the C.U.C. (electricity provider) or the fuel importers comes up. Just mention either and the dark eyes turn red. Steam puffs out of their ears. Feet stomp the ground.

Caymanians from the premier down to the dishwashers are convinced these utilities are the devil incarnate. The C.U.C. (Caribbean Utilities Corporation) and the various gas stations are universally regarded as crooks. Liars. Extortionists. Price-gougers. Evil capitalists. Their crime? They just overcharge compared to similar services in the USA. They have to. Importing energy to a small island in the middle of the Caribbean sea is not cheap. But everyone ignores that detail.

So the natives grumble but the utilities just shrug. You want power or gas, you've got to knock on our door. There's no alternative. The natives buy, but they hate it.

If they thought of it, they might actually arrange the murder of some of the CUC and the various gas stations' directors, but murder is not popular on island. Oh yes, we do have a few a year – no more than four in 2019. But the victims are invariably drunks fighting over ladies, or drunks claiming they were not "respected." You can relax. Tourists are not of interest.

By the way, the police and the courts do not report to the government but to Her Majesty's representative, the governor. A typically wily British trick. Should the "natives get restless," the Crown retains the levers of law and order in its control. The ultimate court of appeal is also British – the Privy Council, in London.

That irks the local politicians a little, but as they contemplate breaking away (Independence!), they look around and see just how badly their independent neighbours have done. Not one can compare in lifestyle, careful financial control, low corruption, GDP, or wealth. So the Caymanians (so far, at least) just grin and bear the long arm of the Crown*** (see more below). And I must say, the Crown generally lets the locals get on with it. Arguably, they are better custodians of wealth creation than their British masters!

*****Two things happened recently which got the "independents" thinking afresh. One, the United Kingdom (UK) supplied the Cayman Islands with an abundance of COVID-19 vaccines, way before anyone else in the Caribbean received any supplies. Two, (and this is an unconfirmed anecdote), a Caymanian politician supposedly went to London and asked under what conditions would the UK grant independence to the island. The reply was short and to the point. "Remember, sir, the Falklands War? If Cuba decided to attack you, and you were no longer an ''overseas' territory', do you think the Royal Navy would rally around?" The politician took the next flight home.

Chapter 14

Keeping Healthy

What do people ask me about when considering moving to Cayman? Well, all sorts of the usual things. Cost of living. Taxes. Safety. Things to do. Real estate. How to get residency and....

Medical competence. If they were to get sick, how good are the doctors and the hospitals?

The answer is, in my experience, as good as I've enjoyed anywhere. Having lived in fifteen of the world's richest capitals, I bet that statement surprises you.

Of course, a small Island of 62,000 folk can't possibly afford all the medical specialists or facilities of a New York, London, or Berlin. But it does have something else. Time. And caring.

Remember that hoary old joke about the old man going to the doctor.

The doctor asks him what's wrong.

The patient answers, "Doctor, Doctor, everyone is ignoring me."

Doctor says, "Next patient please."

There's no danger of that in Cayman. Your Cayman doctor is your friend. He or she takes pride in getting to know you, keeps extensive records, and even follows up on your health by giving you a call from time to time. A session in his/her surgery is not timed to perfection by a body of time-and-motion experts having studied the fastest way to get the most patients through in the minimum time.

No, the Caymanian doctor takes the time, expands the time, and prepares the time to have a detailed session to examine not just the symptoms that brought you there, but the time to learn more about every aspect of your life.

They work with the specialists and the hospitals, not against them in jealous rivalry. They do it all themselves and don't farm out parts of the examination to assistants to save time. It's all a bit old-fashioned, but it works extraordinarily well.

The best eye doctor on island is a rugged Irishman. His schedule is a shambles. He sees a patient and stays with the problem until he has exhausted every possibility. That may have been scheduled for 30 minutes, but if it takes the doctor two hours, tough. The local joke is, if you are not the first patient of the day, take lunch and supper with you. Despite the hour of your appointment, there is no guarantee it will be respected. Even urgent walk-ins can beat you out.

As for hospitals, we have three and two more coming. The national hospital, which is well-respected. Down the road we have a private hospital – the "doctors' hospital" – which is supposed to be better. I've used both. I don't see the difference.

And then we have the latest – Health City – established by the international Shetty organization and erected in the Eastern end of the island specializing in cardiovascular treatment. It is so well-respected that a visiting heart surgeon (who suffered a heart attack whilst snorkeling) stated, "If that had happened in any other part of the Caribbean, I doubt if I would have survived."

Health City also offers so-called extended "medical tourism" facilities, as will two other new hospitals scheduled to open in 2024 or thereabouts. So, by 2025, Grand Cayman should host at least five world-class hospitals in addition to a well-equipped clinic on Cayman Brac.

All these hospitals are - and proposed developments will be - structured to handle any emergency. But if there is a the slightest doubt, air ambulance flights are always available at twelve hours' notice.

Additionally, we have an array of independent experts. Let me give a few examples from my own experience.

My wife contracted a virus in Nova Scotia. She got slowly worse – wouldn't eat or drink, but refused to visit the doctor. "It's just a flu. It will pass." But it didn't. On the fourth day I forced her to visit the doctor. She (the doc) did a series of on-site blood tests and rang back four hours later.

"Michael, get your wife dressed, take your fastest car and race to Health City. They are waiting for you." And they were. Blood tests, scans, spinal taps, and cognitive tests.

Two hours later, the lead doctor called me in.

"Mr Ferrier. The air ambulance is on standby. We are administering a cocktail of anti-viral drugs. She will either respond within 12 hours or we're sending her to Hopkins in Baltimore, the top viral hospital in the USA. If she does not respond to their added drugs, she may well succumb within two days. The virus has climbed up her spinal column and has attacked the brain lining."

Total cost: $7,000. Similar costs in the USA: probably $50,000-plus.

She responded – but it was a close thing.

A visiting relative complained of tingling in his fingers and a neck ache. His local Florida doctor suggested exercise and anti-viral drugs.

On a visit here, I took him to the local neurologist. He immediately feared MS (Multiple Sclerosis). He was right. His suggestion for control was also right. Vegetarian diet, exercise, no stress. The boy is 90% improved.

During the COVID-19 pandemic, the three hospitals tested 65%–70% of the entire population – a world record. At the time of writing, 90% of the over 60's were vaccinated.

So don't worry about medical services. They are as good as I have experienced anywhere. And as I've already mentioned, I've lived in 15 countries. And if the local medical staff believe they don't have the expertise on island, they know where to send you.

One other advantage. Health City is Indian-owned. The canteen (open to anyone) serves the best and most varied Indian dishes on island! Yummy!

Insurance? Unless you can prove conclusively that your international health insurance totally covers you on Cayman, you will be obliged to buy locally. This can be very expensive – unless you opt for the government program, which is very reasonably priced but restricts you to government-approved facilities only, unless those facilities refer you to specialists.

All very neat and tidy and relatively well-managed. Reassuring if you are getting older – as I am!

Chapter 15

Kenneth Dart – Batman of the Cayman Islands

In October 2018, the *New York Times* decided to investigate the man they called the "Batman" or "Superman" of the Cayman Islands. What they meant was that the Islands were receiving enormous financial investment and help from a man they never saw, heard from, or understood.

An enigma, wrapped up in a mystery, as Churchill might have said. And yet Mr Ken Dart is immensely important to the islands' present and future.

So who is this guy and what's his game?

It's hard to get a grip on what motivates him – he's a recluse, and hasn't talked to the press for at least 20 years. He is American, but renounced his citizenship, to the intense annoyance of the US tax man.

His Michigan family either invented or perfected the polystyrene foam containers you use to take excessive food back from a generous dinner. He himself made most of his fortune buying up discounted sovereign debt and forcing payment through court action, and other effective investment vehicles.

He left the USA after a never-explained fire that destroyed his Sarasota dwelling. He chose Belize as his first port of call, but soon locked horns with the government. His right-hand man and investment adviser persuaded him to turn to the Cayman Islands and he has never left the islands since.

His first venture was to establish an upmarket new town a few miles north of the capital called Camana Bay, with residences, condos, office blocks, schools, shops, and restaurants.

Later, his love affair with investing in his adopted home included the famous Ritz-Carlton hotel, a new hotel/condo called The Kimpton, and acres of prime Seven Mile Beach real estate. Soon another hotel - the Indigo - will join the group.

Some say he may own more Cayman acreage than even the government. The locals watch his endless acquisitions with a mix of gratitude and suspicion. Without Dart's continued investment, it is doubtful the islands would have recovered as fast as they did from the devastation of Hurricane Ivan in 2004, which basically flattened 80% of all structures.

Similarly, after the 2008 financial disaster which hit the islands hard, Mr Dart just kept on buying and building.

So why the suspicion? Well, is it arguable that Dart is fast becoming more critical to the islands' future than the traditional administrators. As an example, I was asked to join two government committees. In both cases, I noticed no representation from the Dart companies.

In both cases, the committee chairman indicated that their attendance might dominate the conversation. In other words, many Caymanians are worried about Mr. Dart's growing power and what his ultimate objectives might be.

Based on local estimates, the Dart organisation has probably invested to date nearing two billion dollars. Gossip has it he is planning at least another two billion in developments before he hangs up his hat. Or builder's helmet. One of the most ambitious plans includes updating the rather seedy George Town waterfront and erecting what would become an iconic tower to match the Burj Khalifa in Dubai or the Eiffel tower in Paris.

In my opinion, it is better to invite the bear into your den than have him growling outside – but it's not my island!

So what is Mr. Dart and his organisation's ultimate objective? Frankly, I do not know. Maybe to entice more high-worth individuals to his idea of an Island hideaway. Maybe he is just amused to use his billions to build his own mini country.

Whatever. But we'll never really find out because Mr. Dart is not about to tell us. In my personal view, it was a lucky break that he chose our little island paradise to spend his fortune.

Chapter 16

What's the Future for Cayman?

s you skip through this little book, you probably think I work for the Public Relations Department of the Cayman Islands government. Well, having lived all over the world, I do believe these Islands are hard to beat, and I have tried to tell you why.

Are there dangers ahead? Of course there are. There are dangers for any country at any time, and the Cayman Islands are no exception. But I think the natural pragmatism of the leaders, even as they bicker as politicians must, will keep the hotheads at bay. Extremism is just not the Cayman way. Evolution, not revolution.

What could happen? Well, OK, let's take a look.

The results of COVID-19

The Cayman Islands tackled the virus with brutal efficiency, as we mentioned earlier. They made the omelette, but they had to crack many eggs. The tourist industry is in tatters. Three to five thousand islanders were thrown out of work. The islands' budget surplus is eroded. Will tourism come back and if so, in what form will it return? No one is sure as I write.

The fragile financial industry

The Cayman Islands became the fifth-largest financial centre in the world largely because other centres (like the Bahamas) failed. Pressure from UK socialists or the international financial world could create conditions that squeeze the life out of the island's second-most important industry. I think Cayman is aware of the danger and will cope – but the threat is real.

Taxation

The financial crush of the virus and the pressure of FATCA and others could tempt the government to alter the country's tax-free status. There are rumblings. But wiser minds will prevail. If not, you can kiss the high rollers – the big spenders – good-bye. They can move lightning-fast! One click of a computer and their wealth can be off to Bermuda. Or the Cook Islands. Or Panama.

Independence

There exists a small but persistent minority who dislike being under the ultimate control of a foreign power – in this case, Britain. Brexit, the threat that the Scots might break free, the lack of access to the EU, are creating nervousness. Until now, the decline of other independent former colonies like Jamaica has halted the movement. As has the knowledge that international investors like the fact that a major power is keeping an eye on things. But many Caymanians see their country being overtaken by better-educated expatriates – they want these jobs. They fail to see that if these "experts" go, they take their jobs with them.

Then again, the oldies lament the fact that they can't recognize their islands anymore, dwarfed as they are by new high-rise condos, highways, and disappearing public beaches. Finally, as Europe goes more and more secular, the many vicars, priests, pastors, and even rabbis hate the creeping reach of same-sex unions and social media mockery of traditional religious values.

These items are all risks which could wreck the economy, chase away the investors and high net worth residents, and bring on social unrest.

The antidote, to me, is the lack of extremist politicians or political parties. Without extremist leadership, extremist don't have leaders. A few stupid moves by the motherland (i.e., the UK) could change all that. As could the poisonous influence of Black Lives Matter streaming in from the out-of-control USA – only a one-hour flight away, remember.

The Caymanians never worried about colour, race, or ethnicity. Some of the youngsters now can't escape the daily dump of US negativity streaming through their TV channels.

And, of course, a category 5 hurricane could wreck everything.

These are worries, but I'm not worried. Good old Caymanian common sense has always prevailed for the last 500 years or so.

I think it will still prevail no matter how hard the winds of radicalism may threaten.

Caymanians are the richest in the Caribbean. The best governed. The least contentious and the hardest working.

Who's going to raise the poisoned chalice?

Not I, said the little red hen – one of the thousands roaming our streets and byways, pecking away for the odd insect or crumb.

And that's where this book started. Those chickens delaying our landing at Owen Roberts International Airport those many years ago. Remember?

National Symbols

National Bird - Cayman Parrot

The Grand Cayman parrot is iridescent green with a white eye ring, red cheeks, black ear patches and brilliant blue wing feathers.

National Tree - Silver Thatch Palm

The tall, slender silver thatch palm was an important natural resource for early settlers who used the leaves to make rope, brooms, and roofs.

National Flower - Wild Banana Orchid

The wild banana orchid is the best known of Cayman's 26 species of orchids.

National Flag

The Cayman Islands Flag is a navy-blue field with a Union in the upper left corner and the coat of arms in a white circle.

National Song

"Beloved Isle Cayman" was written by the late Mrs. Leila Ross Shier in 1930.

Coat of Arms

The Cayman Islands coat of arms consists of a shield, a crested helm and the motto. (Three green stars representing the islands. The stars rest on blue and white wavy bands representing the sea. In the top third of the shield, against a red background, is a gold griffin "passant guardant" (walking with the forepaw raised and the body seen from side), representing Great Britain. Above the shield is a green turtle on a coil of rope. Behind the turtle is a gold pineapple, the turtle represents Cayman's seafaring history; the rope, its traditional thatch-rope industry; and the pineapple, its ties with Jamaica. The islands' motto, He hath founded it upon the seas, is printed at the bottom of the shield. The verse is from Psalm 24:2.

National Song

1.

O land of soft, fresh breezes,
Of verdant trees so fair
With the Creator's glory reflected
ev'rywhere.
O sea of palest em'rald,
Merging to darkest blue,
When 'ere my thoughts fly Godward,
I always think of you.
Chorus:
Dear, verdant island, set
In blue Caribbean sea,
I'm coming, coming very soon,
O beauteous isle, to thee.
Although I've wandered far,
My heart enshrines thee yet.
Homeland! Fair Cayman Isle
I cannot thee forget.

The National Anthem

God Save the Queen
God save our gracious Queen!
Long live our noble Queen!
God save our Queen!
Send her victorious,
Happy and glorious,
Long to reign over us,
God save the Queen!

"Beloved Isle Cayman" was written by the late Mrs. Leila Ross Shier in 1930. She became a National Hero in 2021 (January).

National Flag

A popular hike

Ritz-Carlton Hotel – voted one on the best hotels in the Caribbean.

Batabano – Cayman's version of Carnival.

Caymaners love to eat. And meet.

Cayman – culinary capital of the Caribbean.

Thousands of turtles nest on Seven Mile Beach.

Sunset – Cayman is blessed.

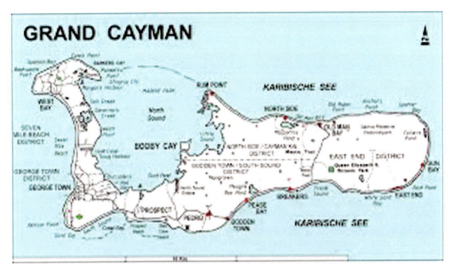

Grand Cayman – largest of the three islands.

George Town – the Capital.

Playing with tame stingrays, at Stingray City

Location of the Cayman Islands.

Caymanite – only found on our islands.

Sculpture made of Caymanite.

Cayman National Museum.

2,300,000 tourists annually can't be wrong!

The family is the core of the Caymanian life

Queen Elizabeth II Botanical Garden.